The Uncommon Wisdom of
Jacqueline Kennedy Onassis

The Uncommon Wisdom of

Jacqueline Kennedy Onassis

A Portrait in Her Own Words

Edited by
Bill Adler
Editor of *The Kennedy Wit*

A CITADEL PRESS BOOK
Published by Carol Publishing Group

A Citadel Press Book
Published by Carol Publishing Group
Citadel Press is a registered trademark of Carol Communications, Inc.

Editorial Offices: 600 Madison Avenue, New York, N.Y. 10022
Sales and Distribution Offices: 120 Enterprise Avenue, Secaucus, N.J. 07094
In Canada: Canadian Manda Group, P.O. Box 920, Station U, Toronto,
    Ontario M8Z 5P9
Queries regarding rights and permissions should be addressed to
Carol Publishing Group, 600 Madison Avenue, New York, N.Y. 10022

Carol Publishing Group books are available at special discounts for bulk purchases, sales promotions, fundraising, or educational purposes. Special editions can be created to specifications. For details contact: Special Sales Department, Carol Publishing Group, 120 Enterprise Avenue, Secaucus, N.J. 07094

Manufactured in the United States of America

10   9   8   7   6   5   4   3   2   1

Library of Congress Cataloging-in-Publication Data

Onassis, Jacqueline Kennedy, 1929-
    The uncommon wisdom of Jacqueline Kennedy Onassis : a portrait in
her own words / edited by Bill Adler.
        p.   cm.
    "A Citadel Press book."
    ISBN 0-8065-1592-9
    1. Onassis, Jacqueline Kennedy. 1929-   —Quotations.
2. Celebrities—United States—Biography.   3. Presidents' spouses—
United States—Biography.   I. Adler, Bill.   II. Title.
CT275.O552O53 1994
973.922'092—dc20
[B]   94-37955
                                                              CIP

We are most grateful to Virginia Fay for her creative efforts in assisting us in putting this book together.

We also would like to acknowledge the research assistance of Doris and Bruce Cassiday, John Malone, Paul Baldwin, and Janet Cavallero.

A Word From the Editor

Much has been written about Jacqueline Kennedy Onassis, but nothing better portrays her—her life, her joys, her tragedies, her courage, her philosophy, and her uncommon wisdom—than her very own words.

—Bill Adler
New York City 1994

CONTENTS

Contents

Contents

The Uncommon Wisdom of
Jacqueline Kennedy Onassis

EARLY LIFE

Childhood

Less than a year after her sister Lee's birth (in 1933), while walking in Central Park with the baby and their nanny, Jackie wandered off. A police officer spotted her alone.

She stepped up to him and said firmly, "My nurse and baby sister seem to be lost."

※

From a childhood poem:
"Oh, to live by the sea is my only wish...."

※

A poem she wrote at age eight:

CHRISTMAS

Christmas is coming
Santa Claus is near
Reindeer hooves will soon be drumming
On the roof tops loud and clear
The shops are filled with people
Snow is coming down
And everyone is merry
In such a busy town.

※

Early Life

Her half sister Janet Jennings Auchincloss was born when Jacqueline Bouvier turned fifteen. She wrote a poem (in the tempo of "The Midnight Ride of Paul Revere,") to commemorate the event:

> Listen, my children, and you shall hear,
> It was nineteen hundred and forty-five
> When Janet Jennings became alive.
> She made all the headlines far and near
> And became the Baby of the Year!
> Crowds to do her homage came,
> Bringing priceless gifts and rare.
> The flower shops all had a boom
> And Western Union tore its hair.

She loved both Merrywood and Hammersmith Farm. While she was at the Sorbonne, she wrote her stepbrother:

"I always love it so at Merrywood—so peaceful—with the river and the dogs—and listening to the Victrola. I will never know which I love best—Hammersmith with its green fields and summer winds—or Merrywood in the snow—with the river and those great steep hills. I love them both—whichever I'm at—just as passionately as I loved the one I left behind."

"I was a tomboy. I decided to learn to dance and I became feminine."
1962, London

School Days

She attended Chapin (elementary) School and was often sent to see the headmistress. Her mother asked, "What happens when you're sent to Miss Stringfellow?"

"Well, I go to the office and Miss Stringfellow says, 'Jacqueline, sit down. I've heard bad reports about you.' I sit down. Then Miss Stringfellow says a lot of things—but I don't listen."

During her high school days at Miss Porter's, she wrote to a Farmington friend:

"I just know no one will ever marry me and I'll end up as a house mother at Farmington."

When she graduated from Miss Porter's in 1947 at age eighteen, she wrote in the class yearbook under *Ambition in Life:* *"Not to be a housewife."*

She refers to a teacher, Miss Helen Shearman (who taught Latin at the Holton-Arms School, where Jacqueline studied for two years), who was somewhat demanding:

"But she was right. We were all lazy teenagers. Everything she taught me stuck, and though I hated to admit it, I adored Latin."

College Days

Jacqueline Bouvier attended college at Vassar (two years), then spent her junior year at the Sorbonne in Paris, and her senior year at George Washington University in Washington, D.C.

During her early college years at Vassar:

"All my greatest interests—in literature and art, Shakespeare and poetry—were formed because I was fortunate enough to find superb teachers in these fields."

During the summer session at the University of Grenoble (a six-week intensive language-arts course prior to the year at the Sorbonne), Jacqueline Bouvier lived with a French family and wrote home:

"They just grow on you so—they get nicer every day and open up to us and treat us like members of the family. We all laugh hysterically through meals and the mother is so good-natured. They are of the old aristocracy and hard up now and have to take in students."

She recalled the kindness of the French students at the University of Grenoble:

"They helped us with our compositions. I wrote mine in halting French and my friend did it all over. It really was very hard and they all took it so seriously and searched for words to use—it was really so nice of them to take all that trouble with some dumb foreigner who couldn't do her homework."

While still in college (senior year at George Washington University), she entered a contest; the prize was a trip to Paris. It required, among other things, writing an essay on "People I Wish I Had Known." She chose Russian ballet impresario Sergey Diaghilev, French poet Charles Baudelaire, and British author Oscar Wilde:

"Baudelaire and Wilde were both rich men's sons who lived like dandies, ran through what they had, and died in extreme poverty. Both were poets and idealists who could paint sinfulness with honesty and still believe in something higher—Diaghileff possessed what is rarer than artistic genius in any one field, the sensitivity to take the best of each man and incorporate it into a masterpiece all the more precious because it lives only in the minds of those who have seen it and disintegrates as soon as he is gone."

From the self-portrait essay written at age twenty-one for the same contest, sponsored by *Vogue:*

"Being away from home gave me a chance to look at myself with a jaundiced eye. I learned not to be ashamed of a real hunger for knowledge, something I had always tried to hide, and I came home glad to start in here again but with a love for Europe that I am afraid will never leave me."

On turning down the Prix de Paris for a year on the *Paris Vogue*, she explained in 1951:

"I guess I was too scared to [go to Paris again.] I felt then that if I went back, I'd live there forever. I loved Paris so much. That's such a formative year when you get out of college, don't you think?"

While studying at the Sorbonne, she and Claude de Renty, the daughter of her landlady, took a trip together in 1950:

"I had the most terrific vacation in Austria and Germany. We really saw what it was like with the Russians with Tommy guns in Vienna. We saw Vienna and Salzburg and Berchtesgaden where Hitler lived: Munich and the Dachau concentration camp—It's so much more fun travelling second and third class and sitting up all night in trains, as you really get to know people and hear their stories. When I travelled before it was all too luxurious and we didn't see anything."

They made several side trips in southern France:

"I just can't tell you what it is like to come down from the mountains of Grenoble to this flat, blazing plain where seven-eighths of all you see is hot blue sky—and there are rows of poplars at the edge of every field to protect the crops from the mistral and spiky short palm trees with blazing red flowers growing at their feet. The people here speak with the lovely twang of the 'accent du Midi.' They are always happy as they live in the sun and love to laugh. It was heartbreaking to only get such a short glimpse of it all—I want to go back and soak it all up. The part I want to see is la Camargue—a land in the Rhone delta which is flooded by the sea every year and they have a ceremony where they all wade in on horses and bless it—La Bénédiction de la Mer—gypsies live there and bands of little Arab horses and they raise wild bulls."

Family

A few summers after her junior year at the Sorbonne, she motored through Italy and wrote her stepfather:

"All the places and feelings and happiness that bind you to a family you love are something that you take with you no matter how far you go."

❊

During the building of her home on Martha's Vineyard in 1981, she spoke to contractor Frank Wangler:

"I've seen the worst of everything, I've seen the best of everything. But I can't replace my family."

❊

Janet Auchincloss Rutherford, her half sister, died at thirty-nine in March 1985 after a battle with cancer. Mrs. Onassis spoke at the service:

"Knowing Janet was like having a cardinal in your garden. She was bright and lovely and incredibly alive."

HER MOTHER

Janet Lee married John B. "Black Jack" Bouvier on July 7, 1928. It was a marriage made in the Social Register. Jacqueline Bouvier was born, six weeks late, on July 28, 1929, at Southampton Hospital on Long Island. Her sister Caroline Lee (called Lee) was born three and a half years later on March 3, 1933. The marriage foundered and the parents separated in 1936, attempted a short-lived reconciliation in 1937, and finally divorced in 1940. In 1942, Janet married Hugh D. Auchincloss. The union produced two children, Janet Junior, born in 1945, and Jamie, 1947. Auchincloss also had three children from previous marriages, Hugh III (Yusha), Nina, and Thomas.

During her junior year at the Sorbonne, Jacqueline told her stepbrother Hugh Auchincloss:

"I have to write Mummy a ream each week or she gets hysterical and thinks I'm dead or married to an Italian."

When her mother and stepfather had been married for a decade, Jacqueline, then twenty-three, wrote a series of poems, each spotlighting an event made possible only by their marriage. Her introduction read:

"It seems so hard to believe that you've been married ten years. I think they must have been the very best decade of your lives. At the start, in 1942, we all had other lives and we were seven people thrown together, so many little separate units that could have stayed that way. Now we are nine—and what you've given us and what we've shared has bound us all to each other for the rest of our lives."

During her courtship days with John F. Kennedy:

"I'm the luckiest girl in the world. Mummy is terrified of Jack because she can't push him around at all."

By the spring of 1954, Jack and Jackie Kennedy, married less than a year, had rented a small town house in Georgetown. They gave small dinner parties at home, on one occasion for eight, including Jackie's mother:

"I think I could entertain a king or queen with less apprehension than my mother, when there are other guests present."

Later, Jack and Jackie purchased a different house in Georgetown and moved in just after the birth of daughter Caroline in 1957:

"Mummy thinks the trouble with me is that I don't play bridge with my bridesmaids."

HER FATHER

John B. "Black Jack" Bouvier was a stockbroker whose finances were as erratic as the stock market. Jacqueline adored her father and they maintained a close relationship, even after her parents separated and then divorced.

Her father often visited her at Miss Porter's School:

"All my Farmington friends loved Daddy. He'd take batches of us out to luncheon at the Elm Tree Inn. Everybody ordered steaks and two desserts. We must have eaten him broke."

A poem written for her father:

> I love walking on the angry shore
> To watch the angry sea
> Where summer people were before,
> And now there's only me.

❖

She once told a friend the one reason she was attracted to Jack Kennedy was that he was "dangerous, just like Black Jack."

❖

A smooth relationship and even compatibility developed between her father and her husband:

"They talked about sports, politics, and women—what all red-blooded men like to talk about."

⁂

Her father died in 1957. She planned his funeral at St. Patrick's Cathedral, with garlands of daisies in white wicker baskets, saying, "I want everything to look like a summer garden."

⁂

Caroline Bouvier Kennedy was born November 27, 1957, four months after the death of her grandfather. Jacqueline regretted that her father didn't live to see his first grandchild:

"He would have been so happy, so happy. Promise me, Jack, that whether it's a boy or a girl, we will give the baby the name of Bouvier."

Her Sister Lee

Caroline Lee Bouvier was born in 1933 when Jacqueline was three and a half years old. She said of her sister:

"Nothing could ever come between us."

 "Lee was always the pretty one. I guess I was supposed to be the smart one."

⁂

"Lee is so dippy about Jack it's sickening," Jacqueline once complained to a friend.

Early Career

In 1952 while working as Inquiring Photographer at the *Washington Times-Herald,* Jacqueline Bouvier, then twenty-two, wrote to newspaperwoman Bess Furman:

"I'm so in love with all that world now—I think I look up to newspaper people the way you join movie star fan clubs when you're ten years old."

She liked to interview children because "they make the best stories." She once interviewed Tricia Nixon, then six. It was right after the 1952 elections, and Nixon had just been elected vice president. Jackie's question was, "What do you think of Senator Nixon now?"

(Tricia's answer: "He's always away. If he's famous, why can't he stay at home?")

In her job as Inquiring Photographer for the *Times-Herald,* her questions showed a whimsical turn of mind:

"Do the rich enjoy life more than the poor?"

"Chaucer said that what women most desire is power over men. What do you think women desire most?"

"Do you think a wife should let her husband think he's smarter than she is?"

"If you were going to be executed tomorrow morning, what would you order for your last meal on earth?"

"Would you like to crash high society?"

"How do you feel when you get a wolf whistle?"

"Are men braver than women in the dentist's chair?"

In retrospect, some queries seem almost prophetic:

"Which first lady would you most like to have been?"

"Would you like your son to grow up to be president?"

"Should a candidate's wife campaign with her husband?"

"If you had a date with Marilyn Monroe, what would you talk about?"

"What prominent person's death affected you most?"

She interviewed Senator Kennedy (whom she was dating at the time) for her column:

"Can you give any reason why a contented bachelor would want to get married?"

Early Social Life

Over lunch, Jack Kassowitz, assistant managing editor of the *Times-Herald* and Jackie's supervisory editor, once asked her to describe her ideal man:

"I look at a male model and am bored in three minutes. I like men with funny noses, ears that protrude, irregular teeth, short men, skinny men, fat men. Above all, he must have a keen mind."

She told dinner companions that the most important thing to her about a man "is that he must weigh more and have bigger feet than I do."

❖

Before she met Kennedy, Jacqueline Bouvier attended parties and dances:
"They were okay. But Newport—when I was about nineteen, I knew I didn't want the rest of my life to be there. I didn't want to marry any of the young men I grew up with—not because of them but because of their life. I didn't know what I wanted. I was still floundering."

❖

During her Inquiring Camera Girl days, her former fiancé (before Jack Kennedy), John Husted, took her to meet his family, and his mother offered her a baby picture of him. She declined, saying:
"If I want a picture of John, I'll take my own."

❖

Separated by geography (Jacqueline worked in Washington, Husted in New York), they corresponded regularly and saw each other on weekends. She had met Congressman Jack Kennedy by this time and subsequently wrote to Husted:
"Don't pay any attention to any of the drivel you hear about me and Jack Kennedy. It doesn't mean a thing."
Shortly after this, they broke off their engagement.

COURTSHIP AND MARRIAGE TO
JOHN F. KENNEDY

Courtship

They first met at the home of Mr. and Mrs. Charles Bartlett in 1951. Congressman Kennedy was planning his campaign for the Senate the following year, and Jacqueline Bouvier had just graduated from George Washington University. The Bartletts brought them together again the following year when Kennedy was actively campaigning for the Senate and Jackie was working as Inquiring Photographer:

"I met him at the home of friends of ours who had been shamelessly matchmaking for a year, and usually that doesn't work out, but this time it did, so I am very grateful to them."

Right after Kennedy's election to the Senate in 1952, her cousin John H. Davis asked her about the rumors concerning Jack and Jackie being serious about one another. She laughed and began describing the senator-elect:

"You know, he goes to a hairdresser almost every day to have his hair done.

"And you know, if, when we go out to some party or reception or something, nobody recognizes him, or no photographer takes his picture, he sulks afterwards for hours.

"Really. He's so vain I can't believe it.

"Oh, sure, he's ambitious all right, he even told me he intends to be president someday."

And she tossed her head back and laughed again.

Of her "spasmodic" courtship, with Jack Kennedy:

"He'd call me from some oyster bar up on the Cape with a great clinking of coins, to ask me out to the movies the following Wednesday."

During their courtship, she once joked to a friend, "I don't know if I'll live long enough to marry him."

Zsa Zsa Gabor recalled meeting Jacqueline Bouvier on a plane flying back from the coronation of Queen Elizabeth in 1953. When they arrived at the airport, Jackie said:

"There's a young man who's going to propose to me."

Unknown to Jackie, Jack Kennedy had once been involved with Zsa Zsa. The actress got off the plane first and greeted him in the waiting room. He introduced the two women.

"Miss Bouvier and I spent hours together on the plane," Zsa Zsa told Kennedy. "She's a lovely girl. Don't dare corrupt her, Jack."

"But he already has," whispered Jackie.

She spoke to a relative about her engagement to Senator Kennedy:

"Aunt Maudie, I just want you to know that I'm engaged to Jack Kennedy. But you can't tell anyone for a while because it wouldn't be fair to the *Saturday Evening Post*."

When asked what the *Saturday Evening Post* had to do with it, she answered:

"The *Post* is coming out tomorrow with an article on Jack. And the title is on the cover. It's 'Jack Kennedy—the Senate's Gay Young Bachelor.'"

⁂

Asked by a reporter at the time of their engagement if she felt she had much in common with Kennedy, she replied:

"Since Jack is such a violently independent person, and I, too, am so independent, this relationship will take a lot of working out."

⁂

She had qualms about the social status of his family:

"Wait till I introduce Jack Kennedy to Aunt Edie [Aunt Edith Bouvier Beale, an eccentric who owned forty cats]. You know, I doubt if he'd survive it. The Kennedys are terribly bourgeois."

⁂

In July 1953, her mother invited Rose Kennedy to Newport for lunch to discuss wedding plans. Jack and Jackie were also there. Before lunch they drove to Bailey's Beach Club. The bride-to-be reported:

"The two mothers were in the front of the car, and we were sitting in the backseat, sort of like two bad children. Anyway, Jack and I went swimming. I came out of the water earlier; it was time to go for lunch, but Jack dawdled. And I remember Rose stood on the walk and called to her son in the water, 'Jack!...Ja-a-ack!' and it was just like the little ones who won't come out and pretend not to hear their mothers calling—'Jaack!' but he wouldn't come out of the water. I can't remember whether she started down or I went down to get him, but he starting coming up, saying, 'Yes, Mother.'"

The Kennedys

THE FAMILY

On her introduction to the Kennedy family:
"Just watching them wore me out."

Commenting on the roughness of the Kennedys' games, she told her sister:
"They'll kill me before I ever get to marry him. I swear they will."

First meeting with the Kennedy clan en masse in Hyannis Port, Cape Cod:
"How can I explain these people? They were like carbonated water, and other families might be flat. They'd be talking about so many things with so much enthusiasm. Or they'd be playing games. At dinner or in the living room, anywhere, everybody would be talking about something. They had so much interest in life—it was so stimulating. And so gay and so open and accepting.

"They even compete with each other in conversation to see who can say the most and talk the loudest."

Responding to the Kennedys' need to be perfect in everything they did, she commented early in their courtship about the game of tennis:

"It was enough for me to enjoy the sport. It wasn't necessary to be the best."

She never did get the hang of the Kennedys' touch football. For her husband's sake, she tried for a while, but she was doomed from the moment she asked, "If I get the ball, which way do I run?"

"The day you become engaged to one of them is the day they start saying how 'fantastic' you are, and the same loyalty they show to each other they show to their in-laws. They are all so proud when one of them does well.

"They seem proud if I read more books, and of the things I do differently. The very things you would think would alienate them bring you closer to them."

She later remembered the Kennedy family (from *Times to Remember* by Rose Fitzgerald Kennedy):

"Something so incredible about them is their gallantry. You can be sitting down to dinner with them and so many sad things have happened to each, and—God!—maybe even some sad thing has happened that day, and you can see that each one is aware of the other's suffering. And so they can sit down at the table in a rather sad frame of mind. Then each one will begin to start to make this conscious effort to be gay or funny or to lift each other's spirits; and you find that it's infectious, that everybody's doing it. They all bounce off each other.

"They all have a humor that's my favorite kind. It's a little bit irrelevant, a little bit self-mocking, a little sense of the ridiculous, and in times of sadness of wildly wicked humor of irreverence. I don't mean they're laughing when they shouldn't be. But to make a real effort to use the light touch when everybody's sad—I think it is wonderful.

"They have been such a great help to me. My natural tendency is to be rather introverted and solitary and to retreat into myself and brood too much. But they bring out the best. No one sits and wallows in self-pity. It's just so gallant that it really makes you proud. And you think, look at these people and the effort they are making, and you think that's a lesson you want to take with you."

Joseph P. Kennedy Sr.

Jacqueline Kennedy became good friends with Joe Kennedy while in Palm Beach during her husband's convalescence from back surgery. Next to her husband and her father, she said of Joe:

"I love him more than anybody—more than anybody in the world."

She was appreciated most by Joe Kennedy Sr. He liked the way she needled him:

"I used to tell him he had no nuances, that everything with him was either black or white, while life was so much more complicated than that. But he never got angry with me for talking straight to him; on the contrary, he seemed to enjoy it."

While the others played football, Joe and Jackie would sit on the porch "talking about everything from classical music to the movies."

She found Joseph Kennedy's old-fashioned slang amusing:

"You ought to write a series of grandfather stories for children, like 'The Duck With Moxie' and 'The Donkey Who Couldn't Fight His Way Out of a Telephone Booth.'"

She defended Joseph Kennedy on charges that he ran his children's careers:

"You'd think he was a mastermind playing chess, when actually he's a nice old gentleman we see at Thanksgiving and Christmas."

Time magazine reported in 1956 that Joe Kennedy had offered her a million dollars to stay married to Jack. When she saw the story, she phoned Joe and said, "Why only one million dollars, why not ten million?"

ROSE KENNEDY

On her first meeting with Rose Kennedy:

"The first time I met her was about a year, a little more than a year, before I married Jack, when I came that summer for a weekend. I remember she was terribly sweet to me. For instance, I had a sort of special dress to wear to dinner—I was more dressed up than his sisters were, and so Jack teased me about it, in an affectionate way, but he said something like, 'Where do you think you're going?' She said, 'Oh, don't be mean to her, dear. She looks lovely.'"

Remembering Rose Kennedy (from *Times to Remember* by Rose Fitzgerald Kennedy):

"When I married Ari, she of all people was the one who encouraged me. Who said, 'He's a good man.' And, 'Don't worry, dear.' She's been extraordinarily generous. Here I was, I was married to her son and I have his children, but she was the one who was saying, if this is what you think is best, go ahead. It wouldn't surprise anyone who has really known her; but anyway, how extraordinarily generous that woman is in spirit. I always called her 'Belle Mère'—and I still call her that.

"She comes and visits us. It's wonderful for Caroline and John. And Ari adores her. The first Easter after we were married she came to spend a few days with us in the Caribbean. That next summer she stopped over in Greece. She was on her way to Ethiopia to have a joint birthday celebration with Haile Selassie. Then, after Grandpa died late that year—I was there in the room with the others when he died—she was feeling sort of shaky. She came and spent New Year's with us.

"If I ever feel sorry for myself, which is a most fatal thing, I think of her. I've seen her cry just twice, a little bit. Once was at Hyannis Port, when I came into her room, her husband was ill, and Jack was gone, and Bobby had been killed…and the other time was on the ship after her husband died, and we were standing on deck at the rail together, and we were talking about something…just something that reminded her. And her voice began to sort of break and she had to stop. Then she took my hand and squeezed it and said, 'Nobody's ever going to have to feel sorry for me. Nobody's ever going to feel sorry for me,' and she put her chin up. And I thought, God, what a thoroughbred."

✳

An old friend recalled a dinner in Paris, while Jackie was married to Onassis, that included Rose Kennedy. Mrs. Onassis insisted that Ari take them to a nightclub:

"You know, Rose hasn't been to a nightclub since Joe took her to the Lido in 1936."

ROBERT F. KENNEDY

After the birth of a stillborn daughter in 1956, Bobby was there for her; her husband was still sailing off Italy. Many years later, she learned that Bobby had also arranged for burial of the child:

"You knew that, if you were in trouble, he'd always be there."

Hyannis, 1960:

"Bobby is immensely ambitious and will never feel that he has succeeded in life until he has been elected to something, even mayor of Hyannis Port. Being appointed to office isn't enough."

She inscribed a leather-bound copy of his *The Enemy Within*:

"To Bobby, who made the impossible possible and changed all our lives, Jackie."

Bobby Kennedy was a great help to Jackie Kennedy and the children:

"I think he is the most compassionate person I know, but probably only the closest people around him—family, friends, and those who work for him—would see that. People of a private nature are often misunderstood because they are too shy and too proud to explain themselves."

During Robert Kennedy's campaign for the Senate, she met with Dorothy Schiff, publisher of the *New York Post,* whose endorsement he needed:

"He must win. He will win. He must win. Or maybe it is just because one wants it so much that one thinks that. People say he is ruthless and cold. He isn't like the others. I think it was his place in the family, with four girls and being younger than two brothers and so much smaller. He hasn't got the graciousness they had. He is really very shy, but he has the kindest heart in the world."

ETHEL KENNEDY

Mrs. Onassis was quoted as saying of Ethel, "She drops kids like rabbits," and she once produced a caricature of Hickory Hill that depicted kids hanging out of windows and underfoot everywhere.

As quoted by Truman Capote, she referred to Ethel Kennedy as "the baby-making machine—wind her up and she becomes pregnant."

Confiding in her sister Lee, she once described Ethel as "the type who would put a slipcover on a Louis Quinze sofa and then spell it Louie Cans."

Courtship and Marriage to John F. Kennedy

EDWARD M. KENNEDY

Wisconsin, 1959:

"Ted is such a little boy in so many ways. The way he almost puffs himself up when he talks to Jack. He hero-worships him, of course. I think it was only last year that Ted started calling him Jack, and I think he first asked if he could. But there's been such a real change in him. He used to be so terribly, terribly serious all the time, but now he relaxes a little more, smiles a little more, and he's still very serious. But he's so very nice and so very intelligent."

JOAN KENNEDY

Jacqueline Kennedy liked Joan Kennedy more than the other Kennedy women did and took her under her wing:

"In the beginning, Joan was so happy with Ted. Whenever we were all in Hyannis Port, you could see the pride on Ted's face when she walked in the room with her great figure and her leopard-skin outfits. If only she had realized her own strengths instead of looking at herself in comparison with the Kennedys. Why worry if you're not as good at tennis as Eunice or Ethel when men are attracted by the feminine way you play tennis? Why court Ethel's tennis elbow?"

JOHN F. KENNEDY

Before their wedding:

"What I want more than anything else in the world is to be married to him."

During their honeymoon, she wrote these lines for JFK:

> He will build empires
> And he will have sons
> Others break down
> When he pursues his course
> He will find love
> Without finding peace
> For it is necessary to search for
> The Golden Fleece
> And all that waits for him
> Is the sea and the wind.

She once compared herself and Jack Kennedy to "icebergs," whose real selves stayed hidden. This "was a bond between us."

After the loss of her stillborn daughter in 1956, she said of her husband:
"He is a rock, and I lean on him for everything. He is so kind. Ask anyone who works for him! And he's never irritable or sulky. He would do anything I wanted or give me anything I wanted."

She didn't see her husband as a typical politician:
"He's an idealist—without illusions."

Preliminary campaign, 1959:

"I married a whirlwind. He's indestructible. People who try to keep up with him drop like flies, including me. It sounds endless and it is. The first two days [of the campaign] were the hardest—but then I got into the rhythm of it."

Jack Kennedy was sometimes called a glamour boy:

"It's nonsense. Jack has almost no time anymore for sailboats and silly things. He has this curious, inquiring mind that is always at work. If I were drawing him, I would draw a tiny body and an enormous head."

Primary campaign, Wisconsin, 1959:

"We didn't talk much when we flew. Jack looked out at the farms and said you could really tell they were family farms, set all apart, all by themselves, and he made a note of it for his next speech at Rice. And he asked Ted Sorensen if he had any jokes. He was always looking for jokes."

In a 1960 Hyannis Port interview, she was asked if her husband was different since becoming a presidential candidate:

"I don't think Jack has changed much, I really don't. He still thinks nothing of answering the door at home when he's wearing his shorts."

During the 1960 campaign:

"If Jack didn't run for president, he'd be like a tiger in a cage."

"Knowing Jack devours twelve hundred words a minute throws me into a state of depression. When we leave here [the White House], he will know everything, and I will be illiterate."

❊

In April 1963, Mrs. Kennedy prepared for the arrival of Grand Duchess Charlotte of Luxembourg. She contacted Basil Rathbone and asked him to present a reading of selections from Marlowe, Johnson, Donne, etc., and the St. Crispin's Day speech from *Henry V*. Rathbone expressed reservations over this latter choice, since it is a monologue about doing away with kings and might be inappropriate for the grand duchess. Mrs. Kennedy wrote and explained:

"It is just one of his [President Kennedy's] favorites for whatever lovely dreams of leading or being led on to victory lurk in his soul. He also knows it by heart and I suppose wanted it for the same selfish reasons I asked for so much Donne and other things I love. He also knows *Henry V* (and he reminds me of him—though I don't think he knows that!)."

A day later she reconfirmed:

"Shall I tell you why I think it is so appropriate?…Of all the speeches that make you care and want to make the extra effort—sacrifice, fight or die—for whatever cause—that is the one. The only person I would not wish you to say it in front of was Khrushchev, as we are not united in purpose—but tiny Luxembourg…we are all striving for the same brave things today."

Rathbone recited the passage.

Early Years of Marriage

From 1957:

"I brought a certain amount of order to his life. We had good food in our house—not merely the bare staples that he used to have. He no longer went out in the morning with one brown shoe and one black shoe on. His clothes got pressed and he got to the airport without a mad rush because I packed for him. I can be helpful packing suitcases, laying out clothes, rescuing lost coats and luggage. It's those little things that make you tired.

"The thing that gives me the greatest satisfaction is making the house run absolutely smoothly so that Jack can come home early or late and bring as many unexpected guests as he likes. Frankly, this takes quite a bit of planning.

"During our first year of marriage we were like gypsies living in and out of a suitcase. It was turbulent. Jack made speeches all over the country and was never home more than two nights at a time. To make matters even more restless, we had rented a house in Georgetown for six months, and when the lease ran out, we moved to a hotel.

"We spent the summer, off and on, at Jack's father's house in Hyannis Port. Ours was the little room on the first floor that Jack used to have by himself. It didn't take me long to realize it was only big enough for one."

"That first year I longed for a home of our own. I hoped it would give our lives some roots, some stability. My ideal at that time was a normal life with my husband coming home from work every day at five. I wanted him to spend weekends with me and the children I hoped we would have."

Then she began to adjust to the pace:

"It was hectic but I loved it. You don't really long for a home of your own unless you have children."

She said later:

"Housekeeping is a joy to me. When it all runs smoothly, when the food is good and the flowers look fresh, I have much satisfaction. I like cooking, but I'm not very good at it. I care terribly about food, but I'm not very much of a cook."

But her refusal to cultivate important people was a source of annoyance to her political husband. At a party, he was overheard saying, "The trouble with you, Jackie, is that you don't care enough about what people think of you."

She snapped back, "The trouble with you, Jack, is that you care too much about what people think of you."

When Senator Kennedy underwent his spinal surgery in October 1954, his wife became his political aide, handling much of his personal correspondence, writing warm notes to dignitaries such as Lyndon Johnson:

"I just wanted to tell you how terribly much your kind letter meant to Jack....I've just realized here I have been scribbling away about my husband's illness and never told you how wonderfully thrilled we are for you being [elected] Majority Leader—You must be so happy and proud—and I know that you will absolutely make history in it."

Referring to Kennedy's recuperation from his back operation in 1954–55:
"I think convalescence is harder to bear than great pain."

In 1954, Bernard Baruch was inadvertently turned away from Senator Kennedy's sickbed by an overprotective nurse, and Jacqueline wrote him:
"If you only knew how crushed we are to have missed you—I know Jack is miserable—because he would have adored to have seen you—but I am sure I am much more—because I would rather meet you than anyone in the world—and now I feel that you are a ship that has passed in the night."

While Kennedy was in New York Hospital after his back operation, his wife was part of a prank in which actress Grace Kelly posed as a night nurse:
"When Jack opened his eyes, he thought he was dreaming. He was hardly strong enough to shake hands with her. He couldn't even talk."

During his convalescence from his back operation, Kennedy worked on his Pulitzer Prize–winning *Profiles in Courage*. She said:
"This project saved his life. It helped him channel all his energies while distracting him from pain."

Commenting on JFK's 1955 bestseller *Profiles in Courage*:
"A sense of history and ability to learn from the past is of prime importance to any man in a position of leadership today."

When an interviewer asked Mrs. Kennedy in 1954 her theories for a successful marriage, she grimly responded, "I can't say I have any yet."

By 1956, after about three years of marriage, she told a reporter:

"I wouldn't say that being married to a very busy politician is the easiest life to adjust to. But you think about it and figure out the best way to do things—to keep the house running smoothly, to spend as much time as you can with your husband and your children—and eventually you find yourself well adjusted....The most important thing for a successful marriage is for a husband to do what he likes best and does well. The wife's satisfaction will follow."

In 1977, the *Boston Globe*'s Virginia Bohlin recalled and quoted from a June 24, 1953, interview given at Hammersmith Farm shortly before the Kennedys' marriage:

"I'm dying to get a place of our own, so I can fix it up myself and get our wedding gifts out of storage. What I hope we'll find is some little Georgetown house. I'd love to have a little cozy house you can really run yourself. Then to furnish it, I'd like some lovely comfortable things mixed in with some nice old pieces of furniture."

Four years later, in 1957, they bought a house in Georgetown and moved in when Caroline was three weeks old:

"I love our home in Washington. There has always been a child in it....My sweet little house leans slightly to one side, and the stairs creak."

Politics

Shortly after their marriage, she spoke to another Senate wife who had attempted to tell her what she was getting into:

"My God. You told me what it would be like, but you really didn't tell me everything. You only told me half."

❊

During the first year of their marriage, it was difficult:

"I was alone almost every weekend. It was all wrong. Politics was sort of my enemy, and we had no homelife whatsoever."

❊

During the early years of their marriage, she had problems grasping the reality of politics that someone was your friend one week and your enemy the next and vice versa.

JFK spoke agreeably about a political colleague he had previously disagreed with. His wife, dumbfounded, would say:

"Why are you saying nice things about that rat? I've been hating him for three weeks now."

❊

However, as time went on, she began to take a different view. Early in 1958, when Jack was a senator, she said:

"Politics is in my blood. I know that even if Jack changed professions, I would miss politics. It's the most exciting life imaginable—always involved with the news of the moment, meeting and working with people who are enormously alive, and every day you are caught up in something you really care about. It makes a lot of other things seem less vital. You get used to the pressure that never lets up, and you learn to live with it as a fish lives in water."

※

In July 1960 when Senator Kennedy was campaigning for president, she said:

"I don't know anything about politics, or didn't until after I got married. Then I heard so much of it all around me all the time that I learned about politics through a kind of osmosis."

※

She also gained a commonsense view of the political life and said on various occasions:

"I separate politics from my private life; maybe that's why I treasure my life at home so much."

※

"In this business there's always going to be flare-ups about something. And you must somehow get so it doesn't upset you. I think I always was fairly good at it. I can drop this curtain in my mind."

※

"I think every woman wants to be needed, and in politics, you are."

※

Sen. Edward Kennedy, in his eulogy at Mrs. Onassis's funeral mass, referring to the visit of the Clintons to Martha's Vineyard the summer of 1993, showed how she had learned the ultimate lesson:

"When we were waiting for President and Mrs. Clinton to arrive, Jackie turned to me and said, 'Teddy, you go down and greet the president.' But I said, 'Maurice is already there.' And Jackie answered, 'Teddy, you do it. Maurice isn't running for reelection.'"

Duties of a Political Wife

Early in their marriage:

"The main thing for me was to do whatever my husband wanted. He couldn't—and wouldn't—be married to a woman who tried to share the spotlight with him. I thought the best thing I could do was to be a distraction. Jack lived and breathed politics all day long. If he came home to more table-thumping, how could he ever relax."

From a television interview during the 1960 presidential campaign:

"The most important thing she needs is to really love her husband. Then, any sacrifices or adjustments she has to make are only a joy."

Mrs. Kennedy had become friends with Mrs. John Sherman Cooper, who gave her several tips she had picked up while campaigning with her husband in Kentucky:

"I remember her telling me that she carried little cards with her, and that whenever she left a city or town, she'd write a note. She told me to do this while campaigning.... Right away when you leave, write a little note, 'Dear so-and-so, thank you for this or that,' because otherwise everything piles up and you forget."

After the 1960 presidential election, she spoke of the role of the political wife:

"You have to do what your husband wants you to do. My life revolves around my husband. His life is my life. It is up to me to make his home a haven, a refuge, to arrange it so that he can see as much of me and his children as possible—but never let the arrangements ruffle him, never let him see that it is work. I want to take such good care of my husband that, whatever he is doing, he can do better because he has me. His work is so important."

Historic Massachusetts made an impression during a campaign swing in 1958:

"I'm so glad Jack comes from Massachusetts because it's the state with the most history. Driving from one rally to another, we'd pass John Quincy Adams's house or Harvard—or Plymouth. I think I know every corner of Massachusetts."

When JFK ran for the Senate in 1958, she made her first campaign speech, telling the Worcester Cercle Français that public speaking in French was "not as frightening as it would have been in English."

1960 Presidential Campaign

Speaking in Georgetown about Senator Kennedy's 1960 presidential primary run against Hubert Humphrey:

"When I saw his schedule of the trip, I told him it was silly zigzagging back and forth, and he agreed. He told me to talk it over with Bob Wallace. I did, and things were changed. That's the first time Jack told me to go ahead and do anything like that."

On providing literary quotes and allusions for Senator Kennedy's speeches:

"I thought of some lines from a poem I thought he ought to use, and he told me to get the rest of it....I used to worry myself sick when Jack said to me that he didn't know what he was going to say in his next speech, but now, even though he still says it sometimes, it doesn't bother me because he has picked up so much more self-confidence in himself and his speechmaking that he can get up without any speech and I absolutely know he'll be all right without fumbling for thoughts or anything because he has so much in his head and he has real presence. I think it's a compliment that I listen to his speeches the way I do because he always has some fresh things to say at the beginning of each speech, things that nobody knows he was going to say. Even in the things he'd said before, the sections of speeches, he always changes them somehow so that each time it's just a little bit different."

On the 1959 presidential-primary campaign trail:

"It's not easy, this traveling, but we are together and he tells me how much it helps him just for me to be there. And I try to be natural with people. I think if you aren't, then they sense it immediately."

In Ashland, Wisconsin, 1959:

"Jack woke me up and Steve [Smith] came in, and while he and Steve were talking about the news stories and things like that, I packed my bag and got dressed. Neither of us is very talkative so early in the morning, especially me. I don't think we said much in the car going out to the airfield. But I remember something in the car going to the airport in Ashford. I saw a crow and I told Jack we must see another crow, and I told him the jingle I learned as a little girl: 'One crow sorrow, two crows joy, three crows a girl, four a boy.' And you should have seen Jack looking for crows until he found more. He would have liked to find four crows. I guess every man wants a boy. But that was a tender thing, I thought."

Campaigning in Marshfield, Wisconsin, before seventy-five people at a luncheon in the Charles Hotel during the 1960 presidential primary campaign:

"We've been working so hard in Wisconsin, and I know that if you do see fit to support my husband, you will find you haven't misplaced your trust. In recent years he has served on the Senate Labor and Public Welfare Committee and in that capacity has done as much for workers in this country as any U.S. senator. He will continue to do everything in his power if elected president."

Ottawa Journal, November 9, 1960:

"Everyone knows campaigning is rewarding. I have seen this country in such detail and every kind of person who lives here; but it is the most grueling thing in the world. It was a life for which I had no preparation."

October 1960:

"This week I made some radio tapes appealing to Puerto Ricans, Mexican Americans, Haitians, and Poles to register and vote. I am grateful to my parents for the effort they made to teach us foreign languages. All these people have contributed so much to our country's culture, it seems a proper courtesy to address them in their own tongue."

"You shake hundreds of hands in the afternoon and hundreds more at night. You get so tired you catch yourself laughing and crying at the same time. But you pace yourself and you get through it. You just look at it as something you have to do. You knew it would come and you knew it was worth it.

"The places blur after a while, they really do. I remember people, not faces, in a receiving line. The thing you get from these people is a sense of shyness and anxiety and shining expectancy. These women who come up to see me at a meeting, they're as shy as I am. Sometimes we just stand there smiling at each other and just don't say anything."

Asked what would happen if her husband lost the nomination:

"I guess it would be like a racing-car driver who is way ahead and winning the race and then someone tells him there is no more gas for his car."

On the campagn trail, 1960:

"If you can't cope with emergencies by the time you're twenty-five, you'll never be able to adapt yourself to situations."

She even charmed the manager of a Kenosha, Wisconsin, supermarket into letting her interrupt his recitation of sale items over the store's loudspeaker. Customers were astonished to hear a soft voice say:

"Just keep on with your shopping while I tell you about my husband, John F. Kennedy."

She went on to talk about his career in the Navy and in Congress, spoke of how deeply he cared for his country, and ended by saying:

"Please vote for him."

During the campaign, she had to answer criticism about her husband's religion:

"I think it's so unfair of people to be against Jack because he's a Catholic. He's such a poor Catholic. Now, if it were Bobby, I could understand it."

Meeting with reporters after her husband got the nomination, Mrs. Kennedy said about her role:

"I suppose I won't be able to play much part in the campaign, but I'll do what I can. I feel I should be with Jack when he's engaged in such a struggle, and if it weren't for the baby, I'd campaign even more vigorously than Mrs. Nixon. I can't be so presumptuous as to think I could have any effect on the outcome, but it would be so tragic if my husband lost by a few votes merely because I wasn't at his side and because people had met Mrs. Nixon and liked her."

While campaigning in Wisconsin, Mrs. Kennedy had gone off by herself to campaign among the black churches. When Senator Kennedy picked her up later in the day, he asked how she did. She said:

"Oh, I did very well. I met the loveliest minister of the loveliest black church, and he has all kinds of financial troubles. I thought it would be nice to help him out, so I gave him two hundred dollars."

JFK said, "Well, that was nice," then on second thought, added, "Goddammit, it wasn't my money, was it?"

※

Pregnancy spared Mrs. Kennedy from most of the 1960 presidential campaign:

"Thank God, I get out of those dreadful chicken dinners. Sitting at head tables where I can't have a cigarette and have to wear those silly corsages and listen to some gassy old windbag drive me up the wall. Poor Jack."

※

At home in Georgetown, pregnant with son John during the 1960 campaign, Mrs. Kennedy hosted women's meetings. She also wrote a syndicated newspaper column, "Campaign Wife.

She discussed her potential role as first lady:

"I wouldn't put on a mask and pretend to be anything that I wasn't."

※

Writing about education and the federal government in "Campaign Wife," 1960:

"Although I certainly agree that education is primarily a local responsibility...it does seem imperative that the federal government step in and do its share.... More teachers must be trained, but... they must be paid more so they will enter the teaching profession."

⁂

"Campaign Wife," 1960:

"Though my child [Caroline] won't even begin nursery school until next year, I worry already about where to send her, all the way through high school, and sound out friends with older children about which school in our area is best for which type of child. Many of them are happy with their children's schooling—but most are not. Several days ago I read that the Prince George's County School Board in Maryland had bought trailers to be used as classrooms to reduce double sessions in elementary schools. It emphasized the urgent need all over the country for additional classrooms. My husband has been deeply concerned with these problems and has recently supported in the Senate a successful effort to pass legislation providing federal aid for school construction and for teachers' salaries."

⁂

Writing about medical care in "Campaign Wife," October 27, 1960:

"Several days ago the Sub-Committee on Medical Care for the Aged released its report for the Women's Committee for the New Frontier. So many people all over the country had written to me about this problem that I was particularly interested in what they had to say. So often this is considered a problem affecting only older people, whereas actually it equally affects those younger people who take care of their parents and sometimes must choose between this and educating their children."

⁂

With only a few weeks left before election day, Jack Kennedy was scheduled to appear in New York and asked his wife to join him.

"If he lost, I'd never forgive myself for not being there," Mrs. Kennedy said, and against her doctor's advice, she went.

⁂

During the campaign luncheon in New York, Jack and Jackie Kennedy were sitting about five seats apart, and she said:

"This is the closest I've come to lunching with my husband in months. I haven't seen him since Labor Day."

⁂

October 1960:

"I am not sure I share the supposed dream of American women to see their sons be president. Being president is one thing. You could not help but be proud of that. But running for office is another—an ordeal you would wish to spare sons and husbands. You worry and wish you could diminish the strain, but of course, you cannot."

⁂

At the end of the 1960 campaign, in Hyannis Port, to John F. Kennedy over network television:

"Jack, I've enjoyed watching this program tonight. I only wish I could have been there with you at the end of this longest and busiest day for you—[the end of] the long road that we've traveled together since the primaries in January. The doctor wouldn't let me leave Hyannis Port tonight so I'll be here until tomorrow morning at six-thirty when I drive to Boston to join you en route. I wouldn't miss it for anything. And then we'll have you back with us at least to wait out the election returns together.

"One of my happiest memories of this campaign has been all of the people who have believed in you, who worked so hard and helped so much. I want to thank all of you who are listening tonight and tell you that we'll never be able to repay our debt to you, and that it is you that we thank tonight with gratitude."

Somebody mentioned it would be good politics to have her baby on the eve of the election:

"Oh, I hope not. I'd have to get up the next day to go and vote."

Election day, November 8, 1960, she informed Arthur Schlesinger that she had cast only one vote—for John F. Kennedy:

"It is a rare thing to be able to vote for one's husband as president of the United States, and I didn't want to dilute it by voting for anyone else."

Pulling out a snapshot of an enormous female rear end bent over so the owner could peer through the Kennedy fence, she told a friend:

"I've got to show you this picture. One of our neighbors took it, and it's my favorite picture of the campaign so far."

To Lady Bird Johnson, Hyannis, 1960:

"I feel so totally inadequate, so totally at a loss. Here I am at the time Jack needs me most, and I'm pregnant, and I don't know how to do anything."

"One day in a campaign can age a person thirty years."

The 1960 Election

John F. Kennedy won the election against Richard Nixon. Mrs. Kennedy was not able to attend all the activities because of her pregnancy and the birth of John F. Kennedy Jr. on November 25, 1960.

"I had been in my room for days, not getting out of bed. I guess I was just in physical and nervous exhaustion, because the month after John's birth was just the opposite of recuperation. I missed all the gala things. I always wished I could have participated more in those first shining hours with Jack, but at least I had given him our John, the son he longed for so much."

Before Kennedy was even inaugurated, there was a threat against his life in Palm Beach:

"We're nothing but sitting ducks in a shooting gallery."

The Inauguration

On President Kennedy's inaugural address:

"I had heard it in bits and pieces many times while he was working on it in Florida. There were piles of yellow paper covered with his notes all over our bedroom floor. That day, when I heard it as a whole for the first time, it was so pure and beautiful and soaring that I knew I was hearing something great. And now I know that it will go down in history as one of the most moving speeches ever uttered—with Pericles' Funeral Oration and the Gettysburg Address."

When they met again for the first time as president and first lady at the Capitol:

"I was so proud of Jack. There was so much I wanted to say. But I could scarcely embrace him in front of all those people, so I remember I just put my hand on his cheek and said, 'Jack, you were so wonderful!' And he was smiling in the most touching and most vulnerable way. He looked so happy."

THE WHITE HOUSE YEARS

The White House

"My mother brought me to Washington one Easter when I was eleven. That was the first time I saw the White House. From the outside I remember the feeling of the place. But inside, all I remember is shuffling through. There wasn't even a booklet you could buy. Mount Vernon and the National Gallery of Art and the FBI made a far greater impression. I remember the FBI especially because they fingerprinted me."

After her tour of the White House with Mrs. Eisenhower, the outgoing first lady, she exclaimed:

"Oh, God. It's the worst place in the world. So cold and dreary. A dungeon like the Lubyanka. It looks like it's been furnished by discount stores. I've never seen anything like it. I can't bear the thought of moving in. I hate it, hate it, hate it."

On her visit to the White House with Mrs. Eisenhower, she told Letitia Baldridge, her new social secretary, that the place looked like "a hotel that had been decorated by a wholesale furniture store during a January clearance."

At first, she disliked the White House, complaining to *Life*'s Hugh Sidey:
"Like a hotel. Everywhere I look there is somebody standing around or walking down a hall."

"I felt like a moth banging on the windowpane when I first moved into this place. It was terrible. You couldn't even open the windows in the rooms, because they hadn't been opened for years. The shades you pulled down at night were so enormous that they had pulleys and ropes. When we tried the fireplaces, they smoked because they hadn't ever been used. Sometimes I wondered, 'How are we going to live as a family in this enormous place?' I'm afraid it will always be a little impossible for the people who live there. It's an office building."

In a 1961 article in *Life* by Hugh Sidey, she is quoted:
"The minute I knew that Jack was going to run for president, I knew the White House would be one of my main projects if he won."

Later in the same interview:
"Like any president's wife I'm here for only a brief time. And before everything slips away, before every link with the past is gone I want to do this. I want to find all the people who are still here who know about the White House, were intimate with it—the nephews, the sons, the great-grandchildren, the people who are still living and remember things about the White House.

"It has been fascinating to go through the building with Mrs. Nicholas Longworth, who was Theodore Roosevelt's daughter, and with Franklin D.

Roosevelt Jr. and President Truman, and hear them tell where things had been placed in their day."

❊

"I just think that everything in the White House should be the best, the entertainment that's given here, and if it's an American company that you can help, I like to do that. If it's not, just as long as it's the best."

❊

"I think the White House should show the wonderful heritage that this country has. We had such a wonderful flowering in the late eighteenth century. And the restoration is so fascinating—every day you see a letter that has come in from the great-great-grandson of a president. It was such a surprise to come here and find so little that had association and memory. I'd feel terribly if I lived here for four years and hadn't done anything for the house."

❊

Privately, she said:

"It looks like a house where nothing has taken place. There is no trace of the past."

❊

She wrote memos to White House staff, this one to J. B. West, the chief usher:

"If there's anything I can't stand, it's Victorian mirrors—they're hideous—off to the dungeons with them. Have them removed and relegated to the junk heap.

"No Mamie pink on the walls except in Caroline's room, no Grand Rapids reconditioned furniture, no glass-and-brass ashtrays or trinkets—I intend to make this a grand house.

"Maud Shaw won't need much in her room. Just find a wicker wastebasket for her banana peels and a little table for her false teeth at night....

"I can't teach the maids anything—nor have time to—when they are that scared, they are too panicky to remember. The only way they will get to be good maids...is to be around the family and house enough so that some of the terror leaves them....

"Something must be done about the window shades throughout the WH. They are enormous and they have pulleys and ropes. After pulling them down I feel like a sailor taking in a sail."

The first spring he was in office, President Kennedy asked Bunny Mellon, an expert horticulturist, to redesign the scraggly patch with flowers just outside his office window. His wife commented on the job:

"It was absolutely atrocious before Bunny took over. Now it's magnificent....The beauty of it seems to affect even hard-bitten reporters who come there just to watch what is going on."

She commented to her decorator, Sister Parrish, about the private living quarters at the White House:

"Let's have lots of chintz and gay up this old dump."

"I never want a house where you have to say to the children, 'Don't touch.'"

Commenting in 1961 on the second-story Oval Room:

"This is a beautiful room. I love it most. There is this magnificent view. It means something to the man who stands there and sees it—after all he's done to get there."

She relished the great view down toward the Mall from the Truman balcony. She told a visitor, sweeping her arm from the Washington Monument to the Jefferson Memorial:

"This is what it is all about. This is what these men fight so hard for."

In 1963, after her husband was assassinated and before she left the White House, she handed out mementos to friends and members of the staff. To Godfrey McHugh she said:

"First I didn't want in, now I can't seem to leave."

Duties as First Lady

Compelled by the 1960 presidential campaign to speak to reporters, this exchange:

"When you are first lady you won't be able to jump into your car and rush down to Orange County to go foxhunting."

"You couldn't be more wrong," Jackie said. "That is one thing I won't ever give up."

"But you'll have to make some concessions to the role, won't you?"

"Oh, I will. I'll wear hats."

The White House Years

When Kennedy won the presidency and Jackie began to panic about her official duties, she told a friend:

"I'll get pregnant and stay pregnant. It's the only way out."

Off the record, she told journalist Charlotte Curtis, her former dormitory mate at Vassar:

"The White House is such an artificial environment. It's a snake pit. If I don't take care of myself, I'll go mad."

On life in the White House:

"What I wanted to do more than anything was to keep my family together. I didn't want to go down into coal mines or be a symbol of elegance. I just wanted to save some normal life for Jack and the children and for me. My first fight was to fight for a sane life for my babies and their father."

She told fashion designer Oleg Cassini that she would "never become stuffy—but there is a dignity to the office which suddenly hits one."

When asked on the *Today* show (September 15, 1960) what the basic duties of a first lady were, she replied:

"I have always thought the main duty is to preserve the president of the United States so he can be of best service to his country, and that means running a household smoothly around him, and helping him in any way he might ask you to."

However, she never liked the title *first lady*:

"It always reminded me of a saddle horse."

And she was less than enthused about the traditional role of first lady:

"Why should I traipse around to hospitals playing Lady Bountiful when I have so much to do around here?"

A year passed and she began to warm to the role:

"I know so much more about it now. Think of this time we're living through. Both of us young, with health and two wonderful children…and to live through all this."

"Sometimes I get furious with myself thinking about all the energy I wasted worrying about what life would be like in the White House. We had such a wonderful home in Georgetown. You'd come in at night and find the fire going, and people talking, and you didn't stay up late. And my fears were that we wouldn't have this anymore in the White House. But that's been the most wonderful side of it. You can talk when he comes home at night. It's better than during the campaign—you don't just dump your bags and go off again. And that's been wonderful for the children. Sometimes they even have lunch with Jack—if you'd told me that would happen, I'd never have believed it.

"But I should have realized, because, after all, the one thing that happens to a president is that his ties with the outside world are cut. And the only people you really have are each other. I should think that if people weren't happily married, the White House would really finish it."

In the late 1970s, Carl Anthony met Mrs. Onassis at the Robert F. Kennedy Memorial Tennis Tournament. They discussed JFK's collection of autographs and letters of historical figures. She asked if he had a collection, and he mentioned that he had every twentieth-century first lady's autograph except Ida McKinley's—and hers. She giggled and said:

"You're going to have a rough time getting in touch with Ida," and gave him her autograph. She asked why he was so interested in first ladies, and he said he was going to write a book about them someday.

A decade later (1987) he did. He sent her an extensive list of questions about her years in the White House.

He sent her the chapters on her in his book, and she made some notes on his manuscript.

He had written: "If there was one sphere where Jacqueline had great influence, it was fashion." She added, "Much to her annoyance."

He used a quote from her on her role as first lady: "She will have an official role, which she must play and accept with grace."

After it she added:

"She had no doubts that she could. Jacqueline Bouvier had been reared in the Puritan ethic of doing one's duty to the fullest and had confidence in her social, administrative and intellectual abilities."

"My stepuncle Wilmarth S. Lewis once told me, 'There were three geniuses of the eighteenth century, and two of them were American— Jefferson, Franklin, and Diderot.' Why shouldn't the White House represent that tradition to the nation and to foreign visitors of state? Why should it not inspire people, make them proud of their country's heritage?"

Life in The White House

She felt she was being hounded by sight-seers and asked for more shrubbery to be planted by the White House fence to obscure the view from the street:

"I'm sick and tired of starring in everybody's home movies."

"We never talked of serious things. I guess because Jack has always told me the one thing a busy man doesn't want to talk about at the end of the day is whether the Geneva Convention will be successful or what settlement could be made in Kashmir or anything like that. He didn't tell me those things. He wanted me as a wife and seldom brought home his working problems—except once in a while the serious ones."

The president left matters of the home to his wife. She once explained to an interviewer:

"When I start to ask him silly little insignificant questions about whether Caroline should appear at some reception, or whether I should wear a short or long dress, he just snaps his fingers and says, 'That's your province.' And I say, 'Yes, but you're the great decision-maker. Why should everyone but me get the benefit of your decisions?'"

She told the chief usher in 1961:

"I want my husband to be able to leave the office, even for a few hours. I want to surround him with bright people who can hold his interest and divert his mind from what's going on over there!"

To J. B. West, the chief usher, after demanding to see the White House bomb shelter, which also served as a command post for the Signal Corps and was filled with people working:

"How amazing! I didn't expect to find so much *humanity!* I thought it would be a great big room that we could use as an indoor recreation room for the children. I even had plans for a basketball court in there!"

The White House, 1962:

"Being in the White House does make friendships difficult. Nobody feels the same. Jack's even more isolated than I, so I do try to have a few friends for dinner as often as possible. Mostly it turns out to be the Charlie Bartletts or Bill Walton or someone we know really well, because I hate to call and have people feel they have to come."

In 1962, after a year in the White House, she said:

"When we first moved into the White House, I was too exhausted at the end of the day to do anything but the state dinners and things we just had to do. Now I'm better organized. I work from eight o'clock in the morning until noon at my desk and try to save lunch and as much of the afternoon as I can for the children."

After the elegance of their visit to France, she decided to have a candlelight dinner on the lawn of Mount Vernon for their next state dinner. Aware of how complicated this would be, she said to the White House usher:

"I suppose you're going to jump off the White House roof tomorrow?"

"No," replied J. B. West, "not until the day after the dinner."

In most ceremonial matters, the president and Mrs. Kennedy came to easy agreement. One night Kennedy summoned aide Chester Clifton to his table in the State Dining Room and muttered a mild complaint about the music the Marine Band was playing. "Let's get something livelier," he said. Clifton went to Jackie and relayed the president's request. "Oh, he does?" she said, surprised. "What does he suggest?" Clifton said the president had in mind some semiclassical numbers. Mrs. Kennedy gave Clifton her most innocent look. "I chose that music myself. But, if he insists, have them play 'Hail to the Chief' over and over. That should amuse him." (Clifton abandoned the mission.)

Old Kennedy pal LeMoyne Billings, JFK's roommate from Choate, visited the White House every weekend. The chief usher always informed Mrs. Kennedy of his arrival:

"Oh, Mr. West. He's been a houseguest of mine every weekend since I've been married."

To J. B. West, after calling him urgently to the White House on a Sunday, his day off:

"There's something brewing that might turn out to be a big catastrophe—which means that we may have to cancel the dinner and dance for the Jaipurs [the maharaja and maharani of Jaipur] Tuesday night. Could you please handle the cancellation for me. This is all very secret."

The next evening, President Kennedy went on television to inform the country of the Cuban missile crisis.

Her husband queried her about the arrival of a dog at the Oval Office, brought by Soviet ambassador Menshikov. The dog, named Pushinka, was the puppy of one of the Soviet space dogs.

"I'm afraid I asked Mr. Khrushchev for it in Vienna. I was just running out of things to say."

To a visitor:

"Look at that Lincoln cake plate. I wonder if there is enough china here to set nine places for tonight. Senator Gore would love to eat off Lincoln's plates."

And that night, Senator Gore did.

(The Senator Gore referred to is the father of the more recent Senator Gore, now vice president.)

❖

During the televised White House tour in the Lincoln Room, Charles Collingwood asked if she spent a great deal of time there:

"We did in the beginning. It was where we lived when we first came here when our rooms at the end of the hall were being painted. I loved living in this room. It's on the sunny side of the house, and one of Andrew Jackson's magnolia trees is right outside the window."

❖

"Sometimes I used to stop and think about it all. I wondered, 'How are we going to live as a family in this enormous place?' I would go and sit in the Lincoln Room. It was the one room in the White House with a link to the past. It gave me great comfort. I love the Lincoln Room. Even though it isn't really Lincoln's bedroom, it has his things in it. When you see that great bed, it looks like a cathedral. To touch something I knew he had touched was a real link with him. The kind of peace I felt in that room was what you feel when going to church. I used to sit in the Lincoln Room and I could really feel his strength. I'd sort of be talking with him. Jefferson is the president with whom I have the most affinity. But Lincoln is the one I love."

A memo to her social secretary dated January 11, 1963:

"I'm taking the veil. I've had it with being First Lady all the time and now I'm going to give more attention to my children. I want you to cut off *all* outside activity—whether it's a glass of sherry with a poet or coffee with a king. No more art gallery dedications—no nothing—unless absolutely necessary."

She was expecting her third child in the fall and wanted to keep the pregnancy secret until April, when the White House would make an official announcement. On trying to keep her pregnancy secret, she told the president:

"I don't know how I'm going to keep this a secret until then. I have an uncanny ability to sense when someone is pregnant, and I just know someone like me is going to find out about it."

Spending

When her husband complained about her spending, she responded:

"I have to dress well, Jack, so I won't embarrass you. As a public figure, you'd be humiliated if I was photographed in some saggy old housedress. Everyone would say your wife is a slob and refuse to vote for you."

During the 1960 campaign for the presidency, she was criticized for spending too much money on clothes:

"That's dreadfully unfair. They're beginning to snipe at me about as often as they attack Jack on Catholicism. I'm sure I spend less than Mrs. Nixon on clothes. She gets hers at Elizabeth Arden, and nothing there costs less than two hundred or three hundred dollars."

Also during the campaign, a New York trade paper contended that Mrs. Kennedy was "too chic" and claimed that she and her mother-in-law Rose spent $30,000 a year buying Paris clothes. She reacted angrily, saying:

"I couldn't spend that much unless I wore sable underwear."

In turn she complained about Kennedy's attempts to control spending at home:

"The president seems more concerned these days with my budget than with the budget of the United States."

During the television tour of the White House, Charles Collingwood asked if all the pieces in the Lincoln Room were from Lincoln's time.

"Yes, they are. The most famous one, of course, is the Lincoln bed. Every president seemed to love it. Theodore Roosevelt slept in it. So did Calvin

Coolidge. It's probably the most famous piece of furniture in the White House. It was bought by Mrs. Lincoln along with the dressing bureaus and chair and this table. She bought a lot of furniture for this house. She made her husband rather cross because he thought she spent too much money."

"I don't understand it. Jack will spend any amount of money to buy votes, but he balks at investing a thousand dollars in a beautiful painting."

The White House Restoration

While President Truman had had the White House repaired structurally, the interior "needed work" by the time the Kennedys moved in.

Mrs. Kennedy resolved to restore the White House to show it at its best: "I want to make this into a grand house."

She spoke to writer Hugh Sidey of *Life,* who was doing an article on the restoration of the White House:

"All these people come to see the White House, and they see practically nothing that dates back before 1948. Every boy who comes here should see things that develop his sense of history. For the girls, the house should look beautiful and lived-in. They should see what a fire in the fireplace and pretty flowers can do for a house; the White House rooms should give them a sense of all that. Everything in the White House must have a reason for being there. It would be sacrilege merely to 'redecorate' it—a word I hate. It must be restored—and that has nothing to do with decoration. That is a question of scholarship."

"When I first moved into the White House, I thought, I wish I could be married to Thomas Jefferson, because he would know best what should be done to it. But then I thought, no, presidents' wives have an obligation to contribute something, so this will be the thing I will work hardest at myself.

"How could I help wanting to do it? I don't know.... Is it a reverence for beauty or for history? I guess both. I've always cared. My best friends are people who care. I don't know.... When you read Proust or listen to Jack talk about history or go to Mount Vernon, you understand. I feel strongly about the children who come here. When I think about my own son and how to make him turn out like his father, I think of Jack's great sense of history."

The president had some misgivings about the expense of the restoration project; she allayed his fears by saying:

"With Henry Francis du Pont in charge of my committee, who would dare be critical? Besides, he's a Republican."

When she was informed that the cost of the White House renovation could create problems, Mrs. Kennedy devised a plan. She invited attorney Clark Clifford to the White House for lunch to get his advice on her idea.

"How many people go through the White House every year?" she asked.

Clifford didn't know, but suggested between one and two million visitors and asked why she wanted to know.

"Before I answer your questions, you answer mine. Do any of these people leave money at the White House?"

"No. The White House is public property. People don't pay to go on the tour. Why should they?"

"They shouldn't," said Mrs. Kennedy. "But we should make available something tangible that they can buy at the White House and take away with them as a memento. We could use the money because, in effect, my goal is to make the White House 'the First House in the Land.'"

Clifford said he'd think about it.

"Don't let's think about it. Let's do something about it," she replied. "I have several ideas. One of them is to sell postcards, not the usual kind but painting postcards of the various state rooms, something the children can take home and paint over. If that's not possible, I want to put together a White House guidebook, a book with eloquent words and beautiful pictures, the kind of publication the *National Geographic* puts out for its members, but not as corny. We'll sell it for a dollar. People who go through this place in fifteen minutes can't possibly tell you what they've seen. This will remind them, and it will help pay for the renovation project. In fact it can be reprinted every time there's a new administration with material included on the ongoing administration."

Mrs. Kennedy eventually established the White House Historical Association to publish the guidebook to sell to visitors. Published with the assistance of the National Geographic Society, it has sold 8 million copies since 1961, with the proceeds used to benefit the White House. Mrs. Kennedy edited the book. The first one was presented to the Kennedys on June 28, 1962.

Jacqueline Kennedy was overheard to say to Chief Usher West:

"Now, J. B., I want it understood that everyone has to pay a dollar, even Ethel."

※

"When I think of all the schoolchildren who come here, I think there should be flowers when there can be, and fires going and the pictures, to make it look rather like a home and not so frightening."

※

She spoke to Hugh Sidey of *Life*:

"I hope the Smithsonian will also maintain a permanent curator at the White House to see that things are properly cared for. For example, the famous Healy portrait of Lincoln in the State Dining Room has a damaged spot that measures eight inches across. Many other presidential portraits are in disrepair. We asked for estimates to restore pictures and frames and the total came to fifty-five thousand dollars. How can we ask Congress to appropriate that much when in these days the money is needed for so many things?

"The White House belongs to the American people. A curator would take care that it is preserved for them."

※

After rummaging through two basements chock-full of White House antiquities, she said:

"I had a backache every day for three months, but it was a new mystery story every day."

Mrs. Kennedy took her duties in the White House restoration project seriously and was enthused about the search for historic items.

Harris Wofford, civil rights adviser to President Kennedy, relates this story:

Kennedy had asked Wofford to bring Martin Luther King Jr. to the White House to discuss the latest civil rights crisis. They got on the elevator, but instead of going up, it went down to the basement and Jacqueline Kennedy entered. She was dressed in jeans and had soot all over her face. Wofford introduced her to Dr. King, and she said:

"Oh, Dr. King, you would be so thrilled if you could just have been with me in the basement this morning. I discovered a chair straight out of the Andrew Jackson era—a wonderful, beautiful chair."

When the elevator reached its destination, she said, "I've just got to tell Jack about that chair."

Then she stopped and said, "But I guess the two of you have other things to discuss."

January 1961:

"The White House is an eighteenth- and nineteenth-century house and should be kept as a period house. Whatever one does, one does gradually, to make a house a more lived-in house with beautiful things of its period. I would write fifty letters to fifty museum curators if I could bring Andrew Jackson's inkwell home."

❖

January 1961

During the restoration of the White House, she suspended afternoon tours, deeming them too disruptive:

"How can they plaster and paint with hundreds of tourists running about?"

Shocked by the poverty she saw while campaigning in West Virginia, she ordered champagne glasses for the White House from the Morgantown Glassware guide.

"That glassware was advertised and sold everywhere as the White House wineglass—it only cost something like six dollars a dozen, but I didn't mind that at all, as I thought it was nice to help West Virginia and nice that people should see that those simple glasses were pretty enough for the White House."

Later, offered a donation of costly glassware, she turned it down and wrote a memo to decorator Sister Parrish explaining why:

"The whole problem is still West Virginia—it still is NO—and will be until they aren't poor any more. It is funny—but in all the places we campaigned—& sometimes I was so tired I practically didn't know what state we were in—those are the people who touched me the most—The poverty hit me more than it did in India—Maybe because I just didn't realize that it existed in the U.S.—little children on rotting porches with pregnant mothers—young mothers—but all their teeth gone from bad diet—I would practically break all the glasses and order new ones each week—it's the only way I have to help them."

Mrs. Kennedy went to great lengths to obtain items for the White House restoration project. She wanted a $10,000 oriental rug for the president's private dining room. She wrote a memo to the chief usher regarding attempted overcharges by antique and rug dealers:

"I so like the rug but we are short of dollars and I am ENRAGED at everyone trying to gyp the White House. Tell him if he gives it he can get a tax donation and photo in our book—if not—goodbye!"

The dealer donated the rug.

In a letter to a mutual friend regarding Mrs. George Henry Warren of Newport:

"I hope that if you ever see Mrs. Warren, you will light a fire under her—as there she is sitting in Newport—with so many houses filled with pretty things and she hasn't even produced one tiny thing. That rather annoys me."

From a letter to Bernard Baruch, February 24, 1962:

"Perhaps you know that we are trying to bring things of past Presidents back to the White House. Someone said that you had an Orpen portrait of Woodrow Wilson. The portrait of him there now is really not all it should be—and I thought it would be the most touching and historic thing if there could be a superb portrait of Wilson—given by you....It is unpleasant to write to friends and to people I admire asking them to part with things they love. If you can't spare the picture I will understand."

Newspaper and magazine publisher Walter H. Annenberg owned a portrait of Ben Franklin that Mrs. Kennedy wanted for the White House. Clark Clifford tells how she telephoned Annenberg and related her plans for making the White House a national monument. She alluded to his priceless art collection.

"I've been told that you have a magnificent portrait of Ben Franklin by David Martin," she said.

Mr. Annenberg began to get the message.

"You, Mr. Annenberg, are the first citizen of Philadelphia. And in his day, Benjamin Franklin was the first citizen of Philadelphia. And that's why, Mr. Annenberg, I thought of you. Do you think a great Philadelphia citizen would give the White House a portrait of another great Philadelphia citizen?"

Although the painting had cost him over $250,000, he did make the donation.

To former Illinois governor and presidential candidate (1952 and 1956) Adlai Stevenson:

"I am just heartbroken to be writing you this because you were so fantastic to respond so quickly and generously to Mary Lasker's pleas—and because it would have been so fitting to have you give the Lincoln settee and chairs—but the sad thing is I got someone to give them—probably the very day Mary wrote to you—as I was so scared we could lose them. I really jumped the gun on myself....I hope Lincoln will forgive me...and that you will too."

During the televised White House tour in 1962, Charles Collingwood pointed out the famous Gilbert Stuart portrait of George Washington:

"That's the oldest thing in the White House. The only thing that was here since the beginning. A rather interesting precedent was set when that picture was painted. A commission was given to the finest living artist of the day to paint the president, and later the government bought it for the White House. I often wish they'd followed that because so many pictures of later presidents are by really inferior artists."

As they toured the Red Room, they discussed the art on the walls:

"I feel so strongly that the White House have as fine a collection of American pictures as possible. It's so important, the setting in which the presidency is presented to the world, to foreign visitors. And American people should be proud of it. We had such a great civilization, yet so many foreigners don't realize it. This little table, for instance; it's by Lannuier, a French cabinetmaker who came to America. Not many people know of him. But he was just as good as Duncan Phyfe or as the great French cabinetmakers. All the things we did so well, pictures, furniture—I think that this house should be the place where you can see them best."

In mid-1966, Mrs. Kennedy responded to a letter from Lady Bird Johnson seeking advice on the continuation of the White House restoration project. Lady Bird was eager to get a new set of china, and Jackie wrote:

"Just a word of warning. Don't let the American china companies do it—I had them trying to copy plates of the Monroe period...from our first days in the White House. The results always looked more like hotel china than the Truman & Eisenhower plates do now....Jansen [in Paris] is the one to do it....Luckily they have a New York office—so one avoids the buying-it-abroad problem....The only other thing I can think of is trying to keep the public rooms—ground and first floor—as 18th and 19th century as possible—so no one in the future will ever change it—and it will remain always a glimpse for Americans back into the days of our country's beginning."

She had another suggestion concerning a donor who had lent the White House some valuable portraits:

"The Fine Arts Committee should threaten, persuade, seduce, coerce him to leave them permanently to the White House, even in his will."

The Relentless Invasion of Her Privacy

During a lull in family conversation, early in their marriage, Jack Kennedy turned to his wife and asked, "A penny for your thoughts."

She replied, "But they're my thoughts, Jack, and they wouldn't be my thoughts anymore if I told them. Now would they?"

All the Kennedys looked at one another; then Joe Senior laughed and said something about liking "a girl with a mind of her own—a girl just like us."

❊

After the 1960 Democratic convention that nominated John Kennedy as its presidential candidate, he flew to Hyannis Port for some badly needed relaxation. An eight-foot wooden fence was built around the Kennedy home to fend off the curious, and a squad of policemen ordered tourists to keep moving. Mrs. Kennedy said softly to Adlai Stevenson:

"I can't bear all those people peering over the fence. Eunice loves the whole horrible business. I may abdicate."

❊

In the hospital after giving birth to John Jr. (November 25, 1960, just after her husband's election), she sat on the hospital sun roof. Another patient wandered by and said, "You're Mrs. Kennedy, aren't you? I recognize you from your pictures."

Mrs. Kennedy answered: "I know. That's my problem now."

❊

Following the birth of John Jr., they went to the Palm Beach home of the elder Kennedys:

"It was so crowded that I could be in the bathroom, in the tub, and then find that Pierre Salinger was holding a press conference in my bedroom."

❊

While she often expressed humor on this subject, she found this invasion of her privacy at times frightening and disturbing. Here are several comments:

At the time of Kennedy's nomination:

"I'm still only thirty years old, and I've just lost my anonymity for good. It's a little scary."

After the 1960 election, she wrote to designer Oleg Cassini:

"PROTECT ME—as I seem so mercilessly exposed and don't know how to cope with it. (I read tonight I dye my hair because it is mousy gray!)"

On the loss of privacy:

"Sometimes I think you become sort of a—there ought to be a nicer word than *freak,* but I can't think of one."

Mrs. Kennedy expounded on the policy of secrecy in a memo to her press secretary Pam Turnure shortly after moving into the White House:

"I feel strongly that publicity in this era has gotten completely out of hand—and you must really protect the privacy of me and my children—but not offend [the press]....My press relations will be minimum information given with maximum politeness....I won't give any interviews—pose for any photographs, etc.—for the next four years."

She had personally researched to find the exact point through the high iron fence around the White House where tourists and news photographers could take photos of the children at play. In a memo to J. B. West, the White House chief usher, she drew a diagram of the lawn:

"If you stand in the children's playground—you will see that lots of people can take photographs from the place marked X."

Then, after asking him if they could have a "solid wall" of trees or shrubs planted there, she continued:

"Who will be the first President brave enough to build a brick wall?"

"When you get written about a lot, you just think of it as a little cartoon that runs along at the bottom of your life—but one that doesn't have much to do with your life."

Dealing With Publicity

A note to orchestra leader Meyer Davis, who played at President Kennedy's inauguration:

"I would very much prefer that you do not use our photograph on the cover of your Inaugural Album—also that you do not reprint my letter. I feel that is commercializing on the Presidency—which is something I will fight against every day of my husband's administration—I should think that if it is written on the back of your album that you played for my mother's wedding and my coming out party and wedding and husband's inauguration—that would be interesting enough for everyone."

Letter to Lawrence F. O'Brien, January 23, 1963:

"I was passing by Mrs. Lincoln's [Evelyn Lincoln, JFK's secretary] office today and I saw a man [Congressman Wayne N. Aspinall] being photographed in the Rose Garden with an enormous bunch of celery. I think it is most undignified for any picture of this nature to be taken on the steps leading to the President's office or on the south grounds. If they want their picture taken, they can pose by the West Lobby. This also includes pictures of bathing beauties, etc."

Jacqueline Kennedy had once been a photographer and had an appreciation for both the technical problems of picture-taking and the use of the pictures. She asked White House photographer Cecil Stoughton:

"Don't make pictures of Jack and me. Make pictures of what we are looking at and what we are doing."

Dealing With the Press

She felt that reporters who were personal friends had no right to ask JFK tough questions. Accompanying him to an appearance on *Face the Nation,* she slipped notes onto the desks of journalists she knew, saying, "Don't ask Jack mean questions."

She found responding to seemingly endless interviews tiresome. She wrote to one editor:

"The thing is—we have done a whole rash of stories lately—four this summer and another coming up [an interview with Richard Rovere for *McCall's*]. The ones we've done are *Life, Look, Ladies Home Journal* and *Redbook.* I am so tired of all the hard work and confusion that goes into a story—especially one with pictures, and feel pretty stale right now....Couldn't you just use some of Jacques Lowe's old pictures—he just took some recent ones of us—trying to get something Jack could use as a Christmas card—please no little photographic essays, Jacques Lowe and I have been through about three sessions like that together—changing clothes, fixing lights, driving to find nice scenery, trying to make the baby smile—I'm sure he wants to avoid it as much as I do!"

Turning down yet another request for a story, she wrote:

"I wish I could either tell you that I would love to do it—or had just been run over by a bus—and couldn't pose for a month. They are marvelous articles—but if you won't be too angry—I think I would just as soon not do one—revealing my few tragic beauty secrets and disorganized wardrobe!"

During the 1958 Senate reelection campaign, she told her stepbrother Yusha Auchincloss:

"Nothing disturbs me as much as interviewers and journalists. That's the trouble with a life in the public eye. I've always hated gossip-column publicity about the private lives of public men. But if you make your living in public office, you're the property of every taxpaying citizen. Your whole life is an open book."

In a note to press secretary Pierre Salinger:

"I thought you had made an arrangement with the fotogs not to take the children playing at WH. They have had all the pictures of [their pony] Macaroni they need. I want no more—*I mean this*—and if you are firm and will take the time, you can stop it. So please do. What is a press secretary for—to help the press, yes—but also to protect *us*." (Italics hers.)

Salinger appealed to the photographers, and for several months they respected her wishes. Then one day the papers were full of snapshots made by an amateur who had sold them to the Associated Press. She wrote another note to Salinger:

"Don't worry—a nice calm memo: Your policy of no peep shows has worked marvelously all fall. Now if they get away with this I am afraid they will start up in full force again. So could you berate the fotog of the AP for buying it—if it was taken by a tourist. Guards should be told to watch for people photographing through grilles. The guards at the gate could have stopped this. If necessary, have one man patrol up and down outside by the S.W. gate."

✷

Jacqueline Kennedy and press secretary Pierre Salinger fought a running battle over publicity, particularly involving the children.

At the end of 1961, she gave him a picture of herself with this inscription:

"From the greatest cross you have to bear."

✷

From a thank-you note during the White House years to a photographer who agreed not to publish photos of Caroline:

"I know that newspapers need to print different—or rather unusual pictures—and there is the conflict of trying to raise one's children fairly normally. So when you—who are torn both ways, respect a little girl's chance to have a happy day with the other children who fortunately treat her as just another 4-year-old (that is almost the only public place where she isn't singled out and fawned over)—it's amazing and consoling."

✷

Mrs. Kennedy wanted the press to be ejected once the White House state dinners got under way:

"That is when they ask everyone questions and I don't think it is dignified to have them around. It always makes me feel like some social-climbing hostess. Their notebooks also bother me, but perhaps they should be allowed to keep them as, at least, you know they are press, but I think they should be made to wear big badges and be whisked out of there once we all sit down to dinner."

In another memo she suggested members of the press "be permitted to attend important receptions but be kept out of sight behind the pillars and potted palms. They are too intrusive. They surround our guests and monopolize them. Nobody could get near John Glenn the other night. Also, the minute the photographers have finished shooting, they are to be ushered out the front door, so the Marine Band can strike up 'Hail to the Chief.'"

※

By order of the president, photographers were barred from taking pictures of her smoking:

"He's such a bear about my smoking that I started encouraging him to have a cigar after dinner. That way he doesn't complain so much about my cigarettes."

Fashion

For the December 1957 issue of *Ladies' Home Journal,* Jackie posed with her sister Lee for a fashion layout. She was quoted (much to her husband's amusement) as saying:

"I don't like to buy a lot of clothes and have my closets full. A suit, a good little black dress with sleeves, and a short evening dress—that's all you need for travel."

※

In a campaign letter in reply to all the unfavorable mail she was getting about her clothes and hairstyle during the 1960 presidential campaign, she said:

"All the talk over what I wear and how I fix my hair has me amused, but it also puzzles me. What does my hairdo have to do with my husband's ability to be President?"

Regarding her inauguration outfit—a beige wool coat with a sable collar and matching sable muff:

"I just didn't want to wear a fur coat. I don't know why, but perhaps because women huddling on the bleachers always looked like rows of fur-bearing animals."

She said to Letitia Baldrige:

"If men only knew how great they looked in their white tie and tails, they would wear them every night of their lives."

Nine days after the 1960 election, she wrote to Oleg Cassini:

"Why don't you get started designing me something? Then send me some sketches. If I like them—I would like to start wearing them about March.

"What I need are dresses and coats for daytime, dresses suitable to wear to lunch. I don't know if you design coats, but I now see that will be one of my biggest problems, as every time one goes out of the house, one is photographed in the same coat.

"Then for afternoon, cocktail dresses suitable for afternoon receptions and receiving lines—in other words, fairly covered up. Also, one or two silk coats to wear over them when I go out in the late afternoon. Any suggestions for accessories you have to wear would also be appreciated.

"Then some pretty, long evening dresses suitable for big official dinners. You know the kind I like: a covered-up look. Even though these clothes are for official life, please don't make them dressy as I'm sure I can continue to dress the way I like—simple and young clothes, as long as they are covered up for the occasion.

"From Christmas to January 20 I will be in Palm Beach in case you might want to send me sketches. After that I will be—you know where— many thanks and best always."

※

She wanted Cassini to consult with her concerning release of information about her wardrobe:

"I don't want to seem to be buying too much.... There just may be a few things we won't tell them about! But if I look impeccable the next four years, everyone will know it is you."

※

Later she wrote to Cassini that she wanted to be dressed as if "Jack were President of France." She knew she was "so much more of fashion interest than other first ladies," but didn't want to be "plagued by fashion stories of a sensational nature." She didn't want to be "the Marie Antoinette or Empress Josephine of the 1960s" and didn't want to "seem to be buying too much." She requested that he "make sure no one has exactly the same dress as I do....I want all mine to be original and no fat little women hopping around in the same gown."

※

By her first official press conference, she spoke of priorities:

"I have no desire to influence fashions. That is at the bottom of any list."

What was at the top?

"Jack."

During her 1962 trip, she visited Buckingham Palace for lunch with Queen Elizabeth II. When she emerged, she diplomatically told the press:

"I thought the queen's clothes looked lovely."

During her trip to India in 1962, the international press criticized her for wearing high fashion in a country overrun with poverty. She instructed her press attaché to refrain from providing further fashion information:

"If you say anything, tell them it's secondhand and that I bought everything at the Ritz Thrift Shop."

Mrs. Kennedy once sent White House photographer Cecil Stoughton to New York to a fashion show. Because her presence at such events proved so disruptive, she asked him to take pictures of the gowns and show them to her. Later she wrote her praise and thanks, adding:

"Don't leave us for *Harper's Bazaar*."

When she was first lady, Mrs. Kennedy had read that her sister was supposedly more elegantly dressed. She wrote to one of her "fashion spies" in Paris:

"What I really appreciate most of all is your letting me know before Lee about the treasures. Please always do that—now that she knows you are my 'scout,' she is slipping in there before me. So this fall, do let me know about the prettiest things first."

Infidelity

Mrs. Kennedy thought she had gone into the marriage with her eyes open. She told a friend:

"I don't think there are many men who are faithful to their wives. Men are such a combination of good and evil."

⁂

She told Joan Kennedy:

"Kennedy men are like that. They'll go after anything in skirts. It doesn't mean a thing."

⁂

Though she was aware of Kennedy's escapades, she never spoke about or confronted him about his affairs, except once when she discovered a woman's undergarment beneath a pillow in the president's bedroom. Holding it between thumb and forefinger, she brought it to him and said:

"Would you please shop around and see who this belongs to? It's not my size."

⁂

When Jacqueline took a French photographer on a tour of the White House, she opened an office door and told the photographer in French:

"And this is a young lady who is supposed to be sleeping with my husband."

✵

There is a story that Marilyn Monroe called Mrs. Kennedy in the White House to tell her she was having an affair with the president. Supposedly she asked how Jackie felt about Marilyn marrying Kennedy, and the response was:

"Marilyn, you'll marry Jack, that's great, and you'll move into the White House and you'll assume the responsibilities of first lady, and I'll move out and you'll have all the problems."

✵

John F. Kennedy was jealous of Mrs. Kennedy's male friends. She was aware of the gossip and told Robin Douglas-Home:

"What can I do? I have dinner with someone, dance with someone for more than one dance, stay with someone, get photographed with someone without Jack—and then everyone automatically says, 'Oh, he must be her new lover.' How can you beat that?"

Humor

Mrs. Kennedy had a great sense of humor and often used humor to diffuse a situation or to lighten things up.

In 1953, at a small party on the yacht of Aristotle Onassis, Senator Kennedy played up to Prime Minister Churchill, but Churchill failed to recognize him. As the young couple left, Mrs. Kennedy eyed her husband in his tuxedo and suggested, "Maybe he thought you were the waiter, Jack."

✵

She once commented to a reporter on how she would occasionally "throw" a long Monopoly game to end it.

The reporter asked if her husband minded.

"Not if I'm on the other side," she answered.

When asked the best site for the 1960 Democratic National Convention, Mrs. Kennedy suggested, "Acapulco."

During the campaign, a reporter asked, "Is your baby due before inauguration day?"

Jacqueline Kennedy said ingenuously, "When's inauguration day?"

Mrs. Kennedy didn't like her husband to bring his work home. According to a White House butler, the president exclaimed, "What in hell am I ever going to do about air pollution?"

Jackie suggested, "It's very simple, my dear. Get the Air Force to spray our industrial centers with Chanel No. 5."

Breaking into a nostalgic conversation at a White House function in 1961 between JFK and Sen. George Smathers, a longtime friend of President Kennedy's:

"Oh, I'll bet you and Jack sit around and talk about those good old days when you fellas used to run around. Well, I guess you fellas would rather be somewhere else tonight."

To a Republican senator opposing a bill JFK favored:

"I thought you were going to be nice to us. If you're not, I won't let you take out Tish Baldridge anymore."

(Letitia Baldridge was Jackie's social secretary.)

❊

She opposed the McCarran-Walter Immigration Act, passed in 1952 over the veto of President Truman. The Kennedy administration was working on relaxing its restrictions:

"A bill that restrictive might not have let in the Bouviers or the Kennedys."

❊

Once during the White House years when Mrs. Kennedy turned up with a new German shepherd puppy, the press asked her what she would feed it.

"Reporters," she answered.

❊

Pablo Casals had played in the East Room. He was superb. Months later, still being complimented on the fact that her husband had done so much for music through the Casals performance, Jackie kidded:

"The only music he really appreciates is 'Hail to the Chief'!"

❊

To August Heckscher, special consultant to the president on the arts:

"Mr. Heckscher, I will do anything for the arts you want....But, of course, I can't be away too much from the children and I can't be present at too many cultural events....After all, I'm *not* Mrs. Roosevelt."

❊

Among the photos taken for the White House guidebook was one of the children in the little boy's bedroom. Everyone liked the picture, but Mrs. Kennedy would not allow it to be used:

"Gentlemen, even at the age of two one's bedroom should be private."

⁂

After she left the White House, her friend Bunny Mellon once gave a birthday party for her. Knowing of her affection for J. B. West, chief usher of the White House, Mrs. Mellon invited him. It was the night before the wedding of Luci Baines Johnson, and he thought it would be impossible for him to be at the party in Osterville, Massachusetts, and get back to Washington in time for the wedding. Mrs. Mellon urged him to come anyway and made all the arrangements. Mrs. Kennedy was very glad to see him and greeted him warmly, then:

"Oh, Mr. West! What's Luci doing without you? If this were the French Revolution, you'd be the first one on the guillotine."

⁂

Referring to photos taken in the 1970s showing her swimming nude off Onassis's island of Skorpios:

"I ought to be flattered."

⁂

After Onassis had died, some would-be kingmakers in New York wanted her to run for the Senate. Her reply:

"If I could do it three days a week."

The Irish

She referred to President Kennedy's Irish "mafiosi" as "the Murph-iosi."
On the day of President Kennedy's inauguration:

"Mrs. Eisenhower said to me in the car on the way to the Inauguration that President Eisenhower looked like 'Paddy the Irishman' in his top hat.' Then she realized she had made a slight gaffe."

As they flew back from Texas after President Kennedy's assassination, she listened to the "Irish Mafia" reminisce:

"How I envied you being in Ireland with him. He said it was the most enjoyable experience of his whole life. I must have those Irish cadets at his funeral. And he loved the Black Watch pipers. They must be at the funeral, too."

She took the children to Ireland in June of 1967 to introduce them to their father's heritage. She spoke to the welcoming crowd at Shannon Airport:

"I am so happy to be here in this land my husband loved so much. For myself and the children it is a little bit like coming home, and we are looking forward to it dearly. I do hope we will come back again and again."

In April 1968, John Walsh became head of her Secret Service detail, leading her to comment in a letter that her entire escort was now Irish along with many of her staff:

"I never imagined that I would become the chatelaine of a band of

Irishmen and women!—but they are the only ones who stay—I suppose it is because the Kennedys are Irish and all Irishmen stick together so much. In my house, everyone has been with me since I moved to New York, except for cooks who wander in and out—and the last one [Annemarie Huste] is now writing a book about working for me and Billy Rose!

"So it is a quality I am particularly grateful for, as I can't have everyone who comes in the door writing a book; the children's English nurse Maud Shaw already did so—and the Irish are loyal enough never to do that—and they get on well together....I know their bad qualities are being too clannish and pugnacious—and I imagine maybe [that's] why...they drive everyone who isn't Irish right up the wall."

Children and Politics

In 1960 she was worried about the effect on the children of their father's nomination and subsequent campaign:

"I worry. All those books on child psychology—and I'm the type who reads all those books—talk about how things affect children Caroline's age. I get this terrible feeling that when we leave, she might think that it's because we don't want to be with her. After the convention, Jack was here for three straight weeks, and Caroline got so used to having Daddy around the house."

Toronto Daily Star, November 9, 1960:

"A big problem in my life...has been that campaigning with Jack has taken me away from home. If Jack proved to be the greatest president of the century and his children turned out badly, it would be a tragedy."

She said upon moving into the White House:

"I want my children to be brought up in more personal surroundings, not in the state rooms. And I don't want them to be raised by nurses and Secret Service agents."

"Raising children is the best thing I've ever done. Being a mother is what I think has made me the person I am."

Mrs. Kennedy once said she personally feels "the most affinity" for Mrs. Harry Truman:

"She brought a daughter to the White House at a most difficult age and managed to keep her from being spoiled so that she has made a happy marriage with lovely children of her own. Mrs. Truman kept her family close together in spite of White House demands, and that is the hardest thing to do."

To Hillary Clinton during a boat ride around Martha's Vineyard, summer 1993—her rule for raising Caroline and John:

"Don't let them have too much attention or be exposed too much, because they deserve a chance to grow up to be who they're going to be."

Her Own Children

Caroline

On November 29, 1957, the day after Thanksgiving, Caroline Bouvier Kennedy was born at New York's Lying-In Hospital, Cornell Medical Center. Three weeks later, wrapped in the same robe her mother had worn at her own christening, Caroline was baptized by Cardinal Cushing at St. Patrick's Cathedral.

Of her husband, Mrs. Kennedy said:

"He is so affectionate with his daughter. She has made him so much happier. A man without a child is incomplete."

During the campaign, Caroline's first spoken words were "goodbye," "New Hampshire," "Wisconsin," and "West Virginia."

Jackie said:

"I am sorry so few states have primaries, or we would have a daughter with the greatest vocabulary of any two-year-old in the country."

To a close friend and parent in 1970 in New York:

"Do you have the same problems with your girls as I have with Caroline? She knows everything and I don't know anything. I can't do anything with her."

At a Christmas party in 1981, Jackie announced:

"I want to introduce you to somebody. I want you all to meet my daughter's new friend, Ed Schlossberg."

Quoted by Carolina Herrera, designer, referring to Caroline's wedding dress design:

"I am not going to get involved because Caroline is the one who will wear it. I want her to be the happiest girl in the world."

John F. Kennedy Jr.

John F. Kennedy Jr. was born on November 25, 1960, just after Thanksgiving, at Georgetown University Hospital, in Washington, D.C. His father had just been elected president.

Just after John F. Kennedy Jr.'s birth, reporters asked if she'd like more children:

"I'd be delighted. I hope that I have many more."

"I don't want the children to be just two kids living on Fifth Avenue and going to nice schools. There's so much else in the world, outside this sanctuary we live in. Bobby has told them about some of those things—the children of Harlem, for instance. He told them about the rats and about the terrible living conditions that exist right here in the midst of a rich city. Broken windows letting in the cold. John was so touched by that he said he'd go to work and use the money he made to put windows in those houses. The children rounded up their best toys last Christmas and gave them away.

"I want them to know about how the rest of the world lives, but also I want to be able to give them some kind of sanctuary when they need it, some place to take them into when things happen to them that do not necessarily happen to other children."

"Caroline is more withdrawn, but John, well, he's something else. John makes friends with everyone. Immediately. He surprises me in so many ways. He seems so much more than one would expect of a child of six. Sometimes it almost seems that he is trying to protect me instead of just the other way around.

"There was that day last November, the day of the anniversary. As the two of us walked home from school, I noticed that a little group of children, some of them from John's class, was following us. Then one of the children said, quite loud, 'Your father's dead…your father's dead!' You know how children are. They've even said it to me when I've run into them at school, as if…Well, this day John listened to them saying it over and over, and he didn't say a word. He just came close to me, took my hand, and he squeezed it. As if he were trying to reassure me that things were all right. And so we walked home together, with the children following us.

"I sometimes used to say to myself, 'He'll never remember his father. He was too young.' But now I think he will. He'll remember his father through associations with people who knew Jack well and the things Jack liked to do. He will be getting to know his father. I tell him little things like, 'Oh, don't worry about your spelling, your father couldn't spell very well, either.' That pleases him, you can bet.

"I want to help him go back and find his father. It can be done. There was that stone his father placed on a mound during his visit to Argentina a long time ago, and then when I took the children there later, John put a stone on top of his father's. He'd like to go back to Argentina and see his stone, and his father's stone—and that will be part of knowing his father."

Patrick Bouvier Kennedy

Patrick Bouvier Kennedy was born five weeks early on August 7, 1963, at Otis Air Force Base, Cape Cod. Suffering from hyaline membrane disease, he was transferred to Children's Medical Center in Boston. He died after only three days of life.

After the death of Patrick Bouvier Kennedy:

"Oh, Jack, there's only one thing I could not bear now—if I ever lost you."

She said later that the president had wanted another boy:

"He felt the loss of the baby in the house as much as I did."

Speaking of the death of baby Patrick:

"That was the only time I ever saw him [JFK] cry. He was inconsolable. As shocking as it was for me, it was worse for him. Jack nearly collapsed over it. Although he never said so, I know he wanted another boy—John was his real kin spirit."

Leaving the hospital after the death of baby Patrick, she thanked the nurses:

"You've been so wonderful to me that I'm coming back here next year to have another baby. So you better be ready for me."

Child Rearing

"It isn't fair to children in the limelight to leave them to the care of others and expect they will turn out all right."

February 1961:

"Children have imagination, a quality that seems to flicker out in so many adults. That is why it is such a joy to be with children."

In 1959:

"People have too many theories about rearing children. I believe simply in love, security, and discipline."

"I always imagined I'd raise my children completely on my own. But once you have them, you find you need help. So I do need Dr. Spock a lot, and I find it such a relief to know that other people's children are as bad as yours at the same age."

On developing creativity in children:

"Perhaps some painting—just some splattering of watercolors or crayon lines the way a child loves to do it—is the first step. Whenever I paint now, I put up a child's paint box for Caroline beside me. She really prefers to dip the brushes in water, smear the paints, and make a mess, but it is a treat for her to paint with her mother.

"Perhaps this will develop a latent talent; perhaps it will merely do what it did for me, produce occasional paintings which only one's family could admire, and be a source of pleasure and relaxation."

"When I was a child, my mother helped us enormously with our creative instincts. She interested us in languages, poetry, and art as young children. She encouraged us to make things for birthday presents instead of buying them. So perhaps we would paint a picture or write a poem or memorize something.

"When I was ten years old, I memorized 'The Vision of Sir Launfal' by James Russell Lowell for my mother's birthday. It was eleven pages long in my poetry book and I was enormously proud of myself at the time. I can still remember whole passages of it today.

"The first year I was married I learned 'John Brown's Body' by Stephen Vincent Benét for my husband, as it was one of his favorite poems and he loved to hear parts of it recited.

"I mention these examples to show that a mind, trained young to retain, continues to do so."

At another point she said:
   "I hope I do as well for my children as my mother did for me."

※

June 1961:
   "As long as the father is the figure of authority, and the mother provides love and guidance, children have a pretty good chance of turning out all right. The family is the prime unit in society. Unless its ties are loosened, children can be properly reared."

※

September 1960:
   "The things you do with your children, you never forget."

※

Ontario Windsor Star, November 15, 1960:
   "Most important, of course, is not to shut off the inquiring mind by being impatient with its questions. The seemingly endless chain of 'whys' means something important to the child—his way of learning."

※

"Children need their mother's affection and guidance and long periods of time alone with her."

※

To a reporter:
   "I was reading Carlyle and he said you should do the duty that lies nearest you. And the thing that lies nearest me is the children."

※

"If you bungle raising your children, I don't think whatever else you do well matters very much. And why shouldn't that be an example, too?"

Art

Mrs. Kennedy once said that the best way to learn to appreciate art is "by using your eyes, by focusing your whole attention on a work of art to try to understand the message the artist wants to convey."

Showing pictures of Lincoln during the television White House tour:
"Here is what the White House did to President Lincoln. Here is how he changed: 1861, the strong man with the arched eyebrow; 1865, one week before his assassination."
The four photographs, one for each year of his presidency, show Lincoln's face aging dramatically.

Regarding the painting of herself she chose for the White House:
"I would have liked it even more lost in shadows. Less specific, more impressionistic."

Travels

During the famous trip to Paris with President Kennedy in June 1961, Mrs. Kennedy told reporters she would have preferred to "walk around and look at the buildings and the streets and sit in the cafés."

Mrs. Kennedy spoke French to Charles de Gaulle, saying, "My grandparents are French."

"So are mine, madame," he replied.

❊

After her return from the trip to France:

"Let me stay as happy as this forever."

❊

Visiting Pope John XXIII in March of 1962:

"He's such a good man—so of the earth and centuries of kindness in his eyes. I was determined to curtsy three times on the way, as you're supposed to do. I did once, and then he rushed forward so I barely got in one more curtsy. I read in the papers I had an unusually long audience, but it didn't seem long. It was all so simple and natural. We didn't talk of anything serious."

❊

After the trip to Vienna in 1961 for a summit meeting with Khrushchev:

"I liked [Mrs. Khrushchev]. She was the kind of woman you'd ask in perfect confidence to baby-sit for you, if you wanted to go out some evening."

❊

During a goodwill trip to India in 1962 with her sister Lee, after a sidesaddle ride on an elephant:

"A camel makes an elephant feel like a jet plane."

❊

On her return to the White House, she said:

"Before we left Washington, I said I wanted to spend one night in a village. The date and the village had been decided upon, but somehow it got out of the schedule. You know, the Indians decided our trip, and I don't blame them. They could have shown me their deepest poverty, hoping I'd go home and say they needed more aid, but they were too thoughtful for that. They just wanted us to have magical memories of an enchanted visit."

Quoted on leaving Hawaii in July 1967:

"I had forgotten and my children have never known what it is like to discover a new place unwatched and unnoticed."

According to I. M. Pei, the renowned architect, when he and Mrs. Onassis visited China together and went to his family's garden in Soochow, he translated something on the wall from the Chinese, and she said, "Why, that's incredible!"

After they returned to the States, she painted a page with a bamboo brush in the classic Chinese manner and put down these words:

"To I. M., who taught me to see fragrance and to read painting."

The Johnsons

During the 1960 presidential campaign, she said:

"Lady Bird would crawl down Pennsylvania Avenue on broken glass for Lyndon."

In a memo to White House chief usher West, she wrote:

"Will you tell whoever it is, after this—at *every* occasion when they play 'Hail to the Chief' & just announce the President—to please also say the Vice President of the United States and Mrs. Johnson—it is so embarrassing to have them not announced & then just disappear like maids."

In a tape made for the Lyndon Baines Johnson Library in 1974, she told Prof. Joe B. Frantz of the University of Texas at Austin:

"One thing Prime Minister Macmillan of England had said to Jack about President Eisenhower and Vice President Nixon—that Eisenhower never let Nixon on the place—impressed Jack a lot. Every time there was a state dinner, he wanted the vice president and Mrs. Johnson to come, too. Once we asked [Luci and Lynda] to a state dinner on their own while their parents were away....You know, young people at that time in their lives should be included in interesting things."

On November 22, 1963, after her husband was assassinated, she was asked by Kenneth O'Donnell if she wanted to watch Lyndon Johnson take the oath of office. She said:

"I think I ought to. In the light of history, it will be better if I was there."

Aboard Air Force One on the way back to Washington, she turned to the new first lady:

"Oh, Lady Bird, it's good that we've always liked you two so much. Oh, what if I had not been there? I'm so glad I was there."

In one of the many deletions requested in the Manchester manuscript *Death of a President,* she is quoted as follows:

On the plane coming back to the White House after the assassination, she contacted Mac Kilduff, assistant White House press secretary:

"You make sure, Mac—you go and tell the president—don't let Lyndon Johnson say that I sat with him and Lady Bird and they comforted me all during the trip. You say that I came back here and sat with Jack."

On the question of whether Kennedy had ever talked about dropping Johnson from the 1964 ticket:

"No, never. I don't think he had any intention of dropping Vice President Johnson."

The day after President Kennedy's funeral, she wrote in her own hand from the White House to President Johnson:

"Dear Mr. president:

"Thank you for walking yesterday—behind Jack. You did not have to do that. I am sure many people forbad you to take such a risk, but you did it anyway....

"Thank you for your letters to my children. What those letters will mean to them later you can imagine. The touching thing is they've always loved you so much. They were most moved to have a letter from you now, and most of all Mr. President, thank you for the way you've always treated me, the way you and Lady Bird have always been to us before when Jack was alive, and now as president. I think the relationship of the president and vice presidential families could be a rather strained one. From the history I've been reading ever since I came to the White House, I gather it often was in the past, but you were Jack's right arm, and I always thought the greatest act of a gentleman that I had seen on this earth was how you, the Majority Leader, when he came to the Senate, was just another little freshman who looked up to you and took orders from you. To then serve as vice president to a man who had served under you and been taught by you. But more than that, we were friends, all four of us. All you did for me as a friend and the happy times we had. I always thought, way before the nominations, that Lady Bird should be the first lady, but I don't need to tell you here what I think of her qualities, her extraordinary grace of character, her willingness to assume every burden. She assumed so many from me, and I love her very much, and I love your two daughters, Lynda Bird most because I knew her the best, and we first met when neither of us could get a seat to hear President Eisenhower's state of the union message, and someone found us a place on one of the steps in the aisle where we sat together. It was strange last night. I was wandering through this house. This is the night after the funeral. There in the East Room, I had framed the page we had all signed, you, Senator Dirksen, Mike Mansfield. Underneath, I had written the day the vice president brought the East Room chandelier back from the Capitol. Then in the library, I showed Bobby the Lincoln record book you gave. You see all you gave, and now you are called on to give so much more. You are the first president to sit in it as it looks today. Jack always wanted the red rug, and I had curtains designed for it that I thought were as dignified as they could be for a President's office. Late last night, a moving man asked me if I wanted Jack's ship pictures left on the wall for you. They were clearing the office for you. I said no because I remembered all the fun Jack had those first days hanging the pictures of things he liked, setting out his collection of whale's teeth, but of course they were there only for you to ask for them if the walls looked too bare. I thought you would want to put things from Texas in it. I picture some gleaming longhorns. I hope you put them somewhere. It cannot be very much help to you your first day in office to hear children out on the lawn at recess. It is one more example of your kindness that you let them stay. I promise they will be gone soon. Thank you Mr. President.

Respectfully, Jackie."

When Mrs. Kennedy was leaving the White House after the assassination, she took Lady Bird Johnson on a complete tour and gave her some counsel:

"Don't be frightened of this house—some of the happiest years of my marriage have been spent here. You will be happy here."

Lady Bird said Jackie repeated that over and over "as though she were trying to reassure me."

When she moved out of the White House on December 6, 1963, she left a handwritten note reassuring Lady Bird Johnson she would be "happy" in her new home. She signed it, "Love, Jackie."

In her oral history provided to the Lyndon Baines Johnson Library, she recalled making several requests to President Johnson:

"I suppose one was in a state of shock, packing up. But President Johnson made you feel that you and the children [could stay], a great courtesy to a woman in distress. It's funny what you do in a state of shock. I remember going over to the Oval Office to ask him for two things. One was to name the Space Center in Florida 'Cape Kennedy.' Now that I think back on it, that was so wrong. If I'd known Cape Canaveral was the name from the time of Columbus, it would be the last thing Jack would have wanted....

"And the other one, which is so trivial, was: there were plans for the renovation of Washington and there was this commission, and I thought it might come to an end. I asked President Johnson if he'd be nice enough to receive the commission and sort of give approval to the work they were doing, and he did. It was one of the first things he did."

After Dallas, Mrs. Kennedy worked hard to polish President Kennedy's image. She told a family friend, journalist Charles Bartlett:

"Bobby gets me to put on my widow's weeds and go down to [LBJ's] office and ask for tremendous things."

Dallas, Texas

She told her friends in early November 1963 that she dreaded the trip to Texas:

"Jack knows I hate that sort of thing. But all he said to me was, 'I'd love you to come with me, but only if you really want to come. You would be a great help to me. But if you don't want to, I will quite understand.' So now I'm quite firm in my decision to go to Texas even though I know I'll hate every minute of it. But if he wants me there, then that's all that matters. It's a tiny sacrifice on my part for something he feels is very important to him."

In Dallas, after the assassination:

"I should not have allowed him to come here. I didn't want him to come here. And he didn't want to come here. Why on earth did they make him come here? Oh, we had so *many* good times."

The summer of 1964 she continued to talk about the assassination, unable to forget:

"I will never go there [Texas] again. You can't imagine how I felt when I was going through Jack's things in the White House and found a set of cuff links in his drawer, emblazoned with the map of Texas. Oh, God—it's awful. I try not to be bitter, but I know I am."

The Assassination of President Kennedy

"My husband never made a sound. He had this sort of quizzical look on his face and his hand was up. I remember thinking he just looked as if he had a slight headache. And then he put his hand to his forehead and fell into my lap."

After President Kennedy's assassination, she was offered a sedative:

"I don't want a sedative, I want to be with my husband when he dies."

Following the assassination, one of the doctors at Parkland Memorial Hospital in Dallas urged her to leave. She said:

"Do you think seeing the coffin can upset me, Doctor? I've seen my husband die, shot in my arms. His blood is all over me. How can I see anything worse than I've seen?"

※

Asked if she wanted to wipe the blood from her clothes:

"Absolutely not. I want the world to see what Dallas has done to my husband."

※

Mrs. Kennedy was determined to spend the night at Bethesda Naval Hospital if necessary:

"I'm not leaving here till Jack goes, but I won't cry till it's all over."

※

At Bethesda, Mrs. Kennedy spoke to her mother:

"He didn't even have the satisfaction of being killed for civil rights. It had to be some silly little communist. It even robs his death of any meaning."

Mrs. Hugh Auchincloss mentioned that the children were safe at her house. Jackie had sent no message to have them taken there.

"Mummy," she said, "my God, those poor children. Their lives shouldn't be disrupted, now of all times." She thought about it. "Tell Maud Shaw to bring them back and put them to bed."

※

She told the story over and over again for the next few days after the assassination. To the White House chief usher:

"To think that I very nearly didn't go. Oh, Mr. West, what if I'd been here—out riding in Virginia or somewhere—thank God I went with him."

✣

Among the many times she showed her concern for the feelings of others at the time of tragedy:

On the Saturday after the Friday assassination, she wanted to contact the widow of J. D. Tippitt, the murdered Dallas police officer:
    "What that poor woman must be going through."

At Bethesda, to Evelyn Lincoln, President Kennedy's secretary:
    "It's getting late and I'm going to be here for a while, so why don't you go home and try to get some rest? You hold up for the next few days, and then we'll all collapse."

Prior to President Kennedy's funeral procession, she reportedly told the staff:
    "Please be strong. In two or three days we'll all collapse."

Pierre Salinger, Kennedy's press secretary, remembers that at the time of the assassination, he had flown all night to get back from an official trip. When he arrived, a Mass was going on in the East Room, and Mrs. Kennedy was there. She came up to him afterward and put her arm around him and said:
    "You know, Pierre, you've had a terrible day. Why don't you spend the night here in the White House."

She said to her social secretary, Nancy Tuckerman, just before leaving the White House in early December:
    "Poor Tucky. You came all the way down from New York to take this

job, and now it's all over. It's so sad. You will stick with me for a little while, won't you?"

The Funeral

After the assassination, she focused on the funeral:
"I don't want any undertakers. I want everything done by the Navy."

At one point, she turned to Angier Biddle Duke, chief of protocol, and said:
"Find out how Lincoln was buried."

Before the funeral, she wrote a letter to her husband and told Caroline:
"You must write a letter to Daddy now and tell him how much you love him."

John F. Kennedy Jr., too young to write, scribbled on Caroline's letter. The letters were put in Kennedy's coffin.

At President Kennedy's funeral, following the eulogies, Mrs. Kennedy led her daughter to the catafalque. Before the cameras, she whispered to Caroline:
"We're going to say goodbye to Daddy, and we're going to kiss him goodbye and tell Daddy how much we love him and how much we'll always miss him."

The family's official literary eulogizer later recorded:
Mother and daughter moved forward, the widow gracefully, the child

watching carefully to do just as she did. Jacqueline Kennedy knelt. Caroline knelt. "You know. You just kiss," whispered Mrs. Kennedy. Eyes closed, they leaned over to brush their lips against the flag. Caroline's small gloved hand crept underneath, to be nearer, and in that single instant an entire nation was brought to its knees. The audience in the rotunda, the national audience, those who until now had been immune, those who had endured everything else were stricken in a fraction of a second. A chord deep in the hearts of men had been touched....Still clutching Caroline, she rose and stepped toward the door with simple majesty. The others stumbled after her."

The march to St. Matthew's Cathedral had been Mrs. Kennedy's idea.
Someone had asked, "What if it rains?"
Her reply:
"Then we'll march under umbrellas."

At the state funeral, as the coffin was being lashed to the caisson, Mrs. Kennedy whispered to her son, "John, you can salute Daddy now and say goodbye to him."

The unforgettable picture of young John, his hand raised in a smart salute, wrenched hearts all over the world.

Shortly after they entered the White House, she had asked her husband where they would be buried.
He had told her, "Hyannis, I guess. We'll all be there." She had said, "Well, I don't think you should be buried in Hyannis. I think you should be buried in Arlington. You just belong to all the country."

Three years later, of course, he was buried at Arlington.

❖

When choosing the spot where President Kennedy would be buried in Arlington National Cemetery, she remarked:

"The place is so beautiful that I could stay here forever."

The Aftermath

In a handwritten letter to Nikita Khrushchev dated December 1, 1963, she wrote:

"Dear Mr. Chairman President

"I would like to thank you for sending Mr. Mikoyan as your representative to my husband's funeral.

"He looked so upset when he came through the line and I was very moved.

"I tried to give him a message for you that day—but as it was such a terrible day for me, I do not know if my words came out as I meant them to....

"You and he were adversaries, but you were allied in a determination that the world should not be blown up. You respected each other and could deal with each other. I know that President Johnson will make every effort to establish the same relationship with you.

"The danger that troubled my husband was that war might not be started so much by the big men as by the little ones.

"While big men know the needs for self-control and restraint—little men are sometimes moved more by fear and pride. If only in the future the big men can continue to make the little ones sit down and talk, before they start to fight....

"I send this letter because I know so deeply of the importance of the relationship between you and my husband, and also because of your kindness, and that of Mrs. Khrushchev in Vienna.

"I read that she had tears in her eyes when she left the American Embassy in Moscow, after signing the book of mourning. Please thank her for that.

Sincerely,
Jacqueline Kennedy"

She told friends she suffered loneliness and despair:

"I'm a living wound. My life is over. I'm dried up—I have nothing more to give, and some days I can't even get out of bed. I cry all day and all night until I'm so exhausted I can't function. Then I drink."

In 1964, the year after the president was shot, she said to Evelyn Lincoln, JFK's secretary, who mentioned the large volume of work:

"Oh, Mrs. Lincoln, all this shouldn't be so hard for you, because you still have your husband.... What do I have now? Just the library...."

She wondered why Mrs. Lincoln needed such a large office to work on President Kennedy's papers and was told that Mrs. Lincoln felt the president's things should be displayed in a nice office. She responded with:

"But these things are all mine!"

She had also questioned what Mrs. Lincoln was actually doing and, when told, responded:

"Why, Mrs. Lincoln, I could sit down and in a half day index all these items on cards myself!"

❊

On November 21, 1965, almost two years after her husband's death, Mrs. Kennedy wrote:

"Learning to accept what was unthinkable changes you."

❊

When she sold Wexford, their house in the Virginia hunt country, she swore the new owners to secrecy, asking them to sign a legal contract prohibiting them from allowing any publicity:

"It's the only house Jack and I ever built together, and I designed it all myself. I don't want it to be exploited and photographed all over the place just because it was ours."

❊

Mrs. Kennedy decided to keep the house at Hyannis Port and gave the following account to Rose Kennedy for her book, *Times to Remember,* published in 1974:

"We spent the first four summers of our marriage with Jack's parents at Hyannis Port. We didn't have our own house here until Caroline was born, or what I mean to say is that's when we moved into it. Grandpa wanted to keep everyone together here. He had this house for us before we lived in it after Caroline was born. I fought against the idea, I thought it was too close, I wanted to be away from the compound.

"But now I am glad. I was reading about a Harvard study of what makes for happy families. Especially what would count most in this age of uncertainty. There were many factors, of course, but close to the top would be a situation in which a number of families knew each other well and had ideas and values they shared, and the children could play at one another's house and sometimes be invited and welcomed for meals. That could happen in a village or small town or a neighborhood, and it's kind of what happens here with the cousins. They're separated more or less most of the year, they live in different cities or different areas of big cities, but they all know one another; and this is the place where they get together, and I think that's awfully important for them.

"The first two summers after I married Ari I wasn't here with the children. Though they were here at times for visits. Then I came back with them for about half the summer.

"And sometimes I think that time heals things...and you forget certain things....I mean, I can't remember Jack's voice exactly anymore...but I still can't stand to look at pictures of him and I don't have any around here except in the children's rooms...and when I came back everything just hit me, because this was the only house where we really lived, where we had our children, where every little pickle jar I had I found in some little country lane on the Cape...and nothing's changed since we were in it...and all of the memories came before my eyes.

"So anyway, after I had looked around and unpacked and all that, the first thing I did was walk over to see her [Rose Kennedy]. And we were sitting and talking about a lot of things, and I said, 'It really hits, doesn't it'...something like that...and that evening she called me and said, would I like to take a little walk around nine-thirty or ten because she didn't want me to be here and alone and be sad. And I thought: 'That woman who has so many reasons to be sad—for her to be thinking about calling me.' It shows you what else she's like. Then the next morning she called and asked me to come and swim with her at such and such a time and…you know, as if she's sort of taking care of me because she thinks I'm in this house by myself with too many memories. So that's what she's like really.

"And I found myself becoming so happy here. The children are happy, and the cousins are here, and all the grandchildren adore her. She's their grandmother and they love her, they're touched by her, they're amused by her, and they respect her. And she does something so clever with them: She sees them in little groups…she'll ask my two over for a lunch or she'll ask herself here for lunch, or she'll see all the Lawfords, or see the three teenage girls, or the little boys who will be interested in fishing, or the college and pre-college ones—and talk with all of them on the level of what interests them—instead of in some great mass scene where they're all tangled little bodies.

"She has the food they like, which is the same food she gave to her children…creamed chicken and Boston cream pie and apple jelly and…in all the years I've known her she's always had the same kind of food, which is the most wonderful, best food there is in the world, sort of American home-cooking food…always the apple jelly and the carrot and celery sticks and the wonderful roast chicken and the acorn squash and the ice cream and cake and all those things that are so good and children love. I think you always like to know that all the best kinds of things are at your grandmother's house."

Camelot

Shortly after President Kennedy was buried, she sat down with author Theodore White for an article to be published in *Life* magazine:

"When Jack quoted something, it was usually classical, but all I could keep thinking of is this line from a musical comedy. At night, before we'd go to sleep, Jack liked to play some records. The lines he loved to hear were:"

She quoted the lyrics from *Camelot:*

> *"Don't let it be forgot*
> *That once there was a spot*
> *For one brief shining moment*
> *That was known as Camelot."*

Then she concluded:

"And it will never be that way again. There'll be great presidents again, but there'll never be another Camelot."

In another interview with Theodore White, December 1963:

"Once, the more I read of history the more bitter I got. For a while I thought history was something that bitter old men wrote. But then I realized history made Jack what he was. You must think of him as this little boy, sick so much of the time, reading in bed, reading history, reading the Knights of the Round Table, reading Marlborough. For Jack, history was full of heroes. And if it made him this way—if it made him see the heroes—maybe other little boys will see. Men are such a combination of good and bad. Jack had this hero idea of history, this idealistic view."

Future Plans

Before President Kennedy's assassination, she had been asked what she would do after leaving the White House:

"I'll just retire to Boston and try to convince John Jr. that his father was once the president."

✻

After the assassination, she had planned to live in Washington:

"I'm never going to live in Europe. I'm not going to travel extensively abroad. That's a desecration. I'm going to live in the places I lived with Jack. In Georgetown and with the Kennedys at the Cape. They're my family. I'm going to bring up my children. I want John to grow up to be a good boy."

✻

She spoke to Dorothy Schiff, publisher of the *New York Post,* during Robert Kennedy's Senate campaign in 1964:

"I don't want to be ambassador to France or Mexico. President Johnson said I could have anything I wanted. I would like to work for somebody, but the list is....One is expecting someone to come home every weekend, but no one....I left Washington because of the old haunts. I just couldn't bear to be reminded all the time. I wanted to move into the house I had lived in when Jack was a Senator, but I could not get it because someone else had it....

"I offered Jack peace, tranquillity, and serenity, but now the board has moved, all the little pieces changed places....People all over ask me to write...there are a lot of requests from magazines, which I've barely looked at....They all want me to write about gracious living or fashion—but I am interested in the same things Jack was interested in."

✻

William Manchester's Death of a President

In early 1964, she and the Kennedy family had asked author William Manchester, a great admirer of President Kennedy, to write the story of the assassination. Manchester agreed to give Jacqueline and Bobby Kennedy editorial control over the completed manuscript in exchange for cooperation. A large percentage of the royalties would be donated to the JFK Library.

Regarding the subsequent controversy concerning *Death of a President*, expressed in her oral history for the Lyndon Baines Johnson Library:

"…in a shell of grief…and it's rather hard to stop when the floodgates open. I just talked about the private things. Then the man [Manchester] went away, and I think he was very upset during the writing of the book. I know that afterwards there were so many things…which were mostly expressions of grief of mine and Caroline's that I wanted to take out of the book. And whether or not they got out, they were all printed around. Now it doesn't seem to matter so much, but then I had such a feeling.

"I know that everybody else wanted the political things unfair to President Johnson out. And the way that book was done—now, in hindsight—it seems wrong to have ever done that book at that time. Don't forget, these were people in shock. Before we moved out of the White House, Jim Bishop was saying he was going to write a book.…All these people were going to do these things, and you thought maybe to just not have this coming up, getting more and more sensational. Choose one person, ask everybody to just speak to him, maybe that would be the right thing to do. Well, it turned out not to be."

※

Mrs. Kennedy fought Manchester on the content of his book, asking for many, many changes and deletions, and she was particularly upset about the serialization in *Look* magazine:

"When my children grow up, I don't want them to read all the gruesome stuff about his brain and the way he looked."

Commenting on the Manchester interviews, she said she spoke freely and in detail because she assumed she was talking primarily "for some scholar in the year 2000."

And that none of it would be used in the book without her express permission, adding:

"I thought that it would be bound in black and put away on dark library shelves."

On November 28, 1966, Mrs. Kennedy wrote to Manchester in London:

"The changes I am talking about...all touch upon things of a personal nature that I cannot bear to be made public. There are many other matters, I know, but these are all of that sort, and they are absolutely necessary to me and my children. I cannot believe that you will not do this much."

✳

She tried to convince Manchester to halt the serialization in *Look* magazine:

"Your whole life proves that you are a man of honor."

Later in the same conversation, she said:

"Anyone who is against me will look like a rat unless I run off with Eddie Fisher."

❊

In January 1967, the case was finally settled out of court when Manchester offered to turn an even larger share of his earnings from the book over to the Kennedy Library.

In 1968, the publisher, Harper & Row, sent a $750,000 check to the library representing the first year's earnings. Mrs. Kennedy issued a statement to the *New York Times:*

"I think it is so beautiful what Mr. Manchester did…all the pain of the book and now this noble gesture, of such generosity, makes the circle come around and close with healing."

❊

On June 17, 1968, she wrote to William Manchester regarding his support of Robert Kennedy's candidacy for president:

"When I read this spring that you were giving your support to Robert Kennedy, I was absolutely startled—then so touched—and much more than that….I want you to know that the last time I saw Bobby alive, we spoke of that. And it meant the same to him….You gave him what he was pleading for [from] others—a wiping off of the blackboard of the past—a faith in now—and a generosity of such magnitude and sacrifice."

Memorials

The day before she left the White House, she ordered an inscribed bronze plaque placed over the fireplace in the president's bedroom, just beneath a plaque commemorating Abraham Lincoln's occupancy of the same room:

"In this room lived John F. Kennedy with his wife Jacqueline during the two years, ten months and two days he was President of the United States."

The plaque was later removed.

On March 17, 1964, Mrs. Kennedy mailed nine-hundred thousand black-bordered prayer cards to acknowledge the sympathy messages she had received:

"I felt St. Patrick's Day was the appropriate time to acknowledge those letters."

She wrote an essay on November 27, 1964, titled "A Memoir," published in *Look* magazine, a year after President Kennedy's death:

"It is nearly a year since he has been gone.

"On so many days—his birthday, an anniversary, watching his children running to sea—I have thought, 'But this day last year was his last to see that.' He was so full of love and life on all those days. He seems so vulnerable now, when you think that each one was a last time.

"Soon the final day will come around again—as inexorably as it did last year. But expected this time.

"It will find some of us different people than we were a year ago. Learning to accept what was unthinkable when he was alive, changes you.

"I don't think there is any consolation. What was lost cannot be replaced.

"Someone who loved President Kennedy, but who had never known him, wrote to me this winter: 'The hero comes when he is needed. When our belief gets pale and weak, there comes a man out of that need who is shining—and everyone living reflects a little of that light—and stores some up against the time when he is gone.'

"Now I think that I should have known that he was magic all along. I did know it—but I should have guessed it could not last. I should have known that it was asking too much to dream that I might have grown old with him and see our children grow up together.

"So now he is a legend when he would have preferred to be a man. I must believe that he does not share our suffering now. I think for him—at least he will never know whatever sadness might have lain ahead.

"He knew such a share of it in his life that it always made you so happy whenever you saw him enjoying himself. But now he will never know more—not age, nor stagnation, nor despair, nor crippling illness, nor loss of any more people he loved. His high noon kept all the freshness of the morning—and he died then, never knowing disillusionment.

"He is free and we must live. Those who love him most know that 'the death you have dealt is more than the death which has swallowed you.'"

"Whenever you drive over the bridge from Washington to Virginia, you see the Lee mansion on the side of the hill in the distance. When Caroline was very little, the mansion was one of the first things she learned to recognize. Now at night you can see his flame beneath the mansion from miles away."

On presentation of the official portraits of John and Jacqueline Kennedy in 1971, Mrs. Kennedy was invited to the White House for the ceremony by Mrs. Nixon:

"As you know, the thought of returning to the White House is difficult for me. I really do not have the courage to go through an official ceremony, and bring the children back to the only home they both knew with their father under such traumatic conditions. With the press and everything, things I try to avoid in their little lives, I know the experience would be hard on them and not leave them with the memories of the White House I would like them to have."

Consequently Mrs. Kennedy and her children came to the White House for a private viewing.

Afterward, Mrs. Kennedy wrote to President and Mrs. Nixon:

"You were so kind to us yesterday. Never have I seen such magnanimity and such tenderness.

"Can you imagine the gift you gave me to return to the White House privately with my little ones while they are still young enough to rediscover their childhood—with you both as guides—and with your daughters, such extraordinary young women.

"What a tribute to have brought them up like that in the limelight. I pray I can do half the same with my Caroline. It was good to see her exposed to their example, and John to their charm!

"Thank you with all my heart. A day I always dreaded turned out to be one of the most precious ones I have spent with my children."

John F. Kennedy Library

An exhibit of President Kennedy's mementos was to tour the country to raise funds for the Kennedy Library to be built at Harvard:

"I have added some books which he always kept in the Oval Room in the White House. He had them when we were married, and they, too, give an insight to what he really loved.

"There are books which he read and reread on some of the American statesmen, such as Clay, Calhoun, Webster, John Randolph, and John Quincy Adams. I hope that young people will be interested in seeing these books which the president loved, and that like him they will read American history."

·⁜·

She spoke the above words in January 1964. In May of that year she announced the start of the touring exhibit for the Library, which would open in Boston in 1979:

"I want to take this opportunity to express my appreciation for the hundreds of thousands of messages...which my children and I have received over the past few weeks.

"The knowledge of the affection in which my husband was held by all of you has sustained me, and the warmth of these tributes is something I shall never forget. Whenever I can bear to, I read them. All his bright light gone from the world. All of you who have written to me know how much we all loved him and that he returned that love in full measure.

"It is my greatest wish that all of these letters be acknowledged. They will be, but it will take a long time to do so....I know you will understand.

"Each and every message is to be treasured, not only for my children, but so that future generations will know how much our country and people in other nations thought of him. Your letters will be placed with his papers in the library to be erected in his memory. I hope that in years to come many of you and your children will be able to visit the Kennedy Library. It will be, we hope, not only a memorial...but a living center of study...for young people and for scholars from all over the world.

"May I thank you again on behalf of my children and of the president's family for the comfort that your letters have brought to us all."

⁂

Mrs. Kennedy made a film for the exhibit to raise money for the JFK Library. She was nervous appearing before the camera:

"I wish I knew when to breathe. I just don't see how actresses can do this."

Memories

Mrs. Kennedy moved back to Georgetown after the assassination. She wanted to maintain continuity for the children, and she asked her husband's special assistant David Powers to play soldier with John, as he used to do in the White House:

"He'll remember his father through associations with people who knew Jack well."

⁂

After the assassination, busloads of tourists arrived at her home in Georgetown:

"They actually sit there and eat their lunch and throw sandwich wrappers on the ground. I'm trapped in that house and can't get out. I can't even change my clothes in private because they can look in my bedroom window."

⁂

"One must not let oneself be overwhelmed by sadness."

⁂

To Joan Braden, wife of newspaper publisher Tom Braden:

"There'll never be another Jack. I now understand why he lived so intensely and on the brink. And I'm glad he did."

After leaving the White House, she met with decorator Billy Baldwin to discuss decorating her new house in Georgetown. She showed him pieces of Greek sculpture and Roman fragments:

"I have some beautiful things to show you. These are the beginnings of a collection Jack started. It's so sad to be doing this. Like a young married couple fixing up their first house together. I could never make the White House personal...."

She became tearful. "Oh, Mr. Baldwin, I'm afraid I'm going to embarrass you. I just can't hold it in any longer." She buried her face in her hands and wept. Later she continued, "I know from my very brief acquaintance with you that you are a sympathetic man. Do you mind if I tell you something? I know my husband was devoted to me. I know he was proud of me. It took a very long time for us to work everything out, but we did, and we were about to have a real life together. I was going to campaign with him. I know I held a very special place for him—a unique place...." She talked on about JFK and their life. "Can anyone understand how it is to have lived in the White House and then, suddenly, to be living alone as the president's widow? There is something so final about it. And the children. The world is pouring terrible adoration at the feet of my children and I fear for them, for this awful exposure. How can I bring them up normally? We would never even have named John after his father if we had known...."

She sent a photograph of herself with the president to Mrs. Tippitt, widow of the police officer shot by Oswald in Dallas, and inscribed it:

"There is another bond we share. We must remind our children all the time what brave men their fathers were."

In 1964, to a photographer who had taken happy family pictures at Hyannis Port:

"Remember then we said the pictures would be so wonderful for the children to look at twenty years from now. But who could know?"

Glen Ora, 1964:

"I try not to be bitter. I never had or wanted a life of my own. Everything centered around Jack. I can't believe that I'll never see him again. Sometimes I wake in the morning, eager to tell him something, and he's not there....Nearly every religion teaches there's an afterlife, and I cling to that hope. Those three years we spent in the White House were really the happiest time for us, the closest, and now it's all gone. Now there is nothing, nothing."

She spoke to her personal secretary Mary Gallagher in early December 1963:

"Why did Jack have to die so young? Even when you're sixty, you like to know your husband is there. It's so hard for the children. Please, Mary, don't ever leave. Get yourself fixed for salary on my government appropriation—just don't leave me!"

(She later dismissed her secretary when she moved to New York.)

"The world has no right to Jack's private life with me. I shared all these rooms with him, not with the Book-of-the-Month Club readers, and I don't want them shopping through those rooms now."

White House, 1964:
  "He lived at such a pace because he wished to know it all."

She spoke with *New York Post* publisher Dorothy Schiff during Robert Kennedy's senatorial campaign in 1964:
  "People tell me that time will heal. How much time? Last week I forgot to cancel the newspapers and I picked them up and there was the publication of the Warren Report, so I canceled them for the rest of the week. But I went to the hairdresser and picked up *Life* magazine and it was terrible. There is November to be gotten through....Maybe by the first of the year...."

Summer 1964:
  "I was so fiercely loyal to him I once said thoughtlessly he should be president for life! No, he said, even if he were reelected, eight years in the Presidency is enough for any man.

In March 1964, she showed Richard B. Stolley of *Life* a photo taken from behind her, President Kennedy, and the children:

"That was only nine days before Jack was killed. It was the only picture I could have around for months. I just couldn't look at his face."

To Dorothy Schiff of the *New York Post*, she reminisced:

"I never told him anything or showed him anything unpleasant, and when he got home, I always had his favorite drink, a daiquiri, ready for him, and his favorite record playing, and perhaps a few friends."

After the 1964 convention, she informed Bobby Kennedy that she had no intention of voting in the forthcoming election:

"I'm not going to vote for any other person, because this vote would have been his."

New York, 1964:

"Most men don't care about children as much as women do, but [Jack] did. He was the kind of man who should have had a brood of children."

⁂

Her hairdresser at Kenneth's remembers the first anniversary of John F. Kennedy's assassination. Down Fifth Avenue there were pictures of him in every store window. Mrs. Kennedy arrived, broke down, and sobbed:

"Oh, Rosemary, it was so awful in Washington. They'd follow me everywhere and sit out there in front of the house all day and eat their lunch and throw papers on the lawn. I thought that moving to New York would make it easier for me. If God had only let my baby live. I walk down the street and see his picture in every window. I can't stand it. Why do they remember the assassination? Why can't they celebrate his birthday?"

She told a relative in 1964 that no matter what she did she felt overshadowed by death:

"I can't escape it. Whether I'm helping with the Kennedy Memorial at Harvard or taking a plane from Kennedy Airport or seeing a Kennedy in-law, I always think of Jack and what they did to him."

Assassination of Robert F. Kennedy

By April 1968, Robert Kennedy had decided to run for president. At a New York dinner party that month, Jacqueline Kennedy took the historian Arthur Schlesinger aside and said:

"Do you know what I think will happen to Bobby? The same thing that happened to Jack....There is so much hatred in this country, and more people hate Bobby than hated Jack....I've told Bobby this, but he isn't fatalistic, like me."

✳

After Robert Kennedy's death, she went to the hospital in Los Angeles and spoke to Bobby's press secretary, Frank Mankiewicz:

"The Church is...at its best only at the time of death. The rest of the time it's often rather silly little men running around in their black suits. But the Catholic Church understands death. I'll tell you who else understands death are the black churches. I remember at the funeral of Martin Luther King. I was looking at those faces, and I realized that they know death. They see it all the time and they're ready for it…in the way in which a good Catholic is. We know death.…As a matter of fact, if it weren't for the children, we'd welcome it."

Security

After President Kennedy was killed, Mrs. Kennedy took the children to live in New York. Danger was never far from her mind, and she once confided to a teacher:

"I'm nerve-wracked about the safety of the children. There are so many nut cases about."

❊

After the assassinations of Robert Kennedy and Martin Luther King Jr., she told a friend:

"I despise America and I don't want my children to live here anymore. If they're killing Kennedys, my kids are number-one targets.…I want to get out of this country."

❊

Mrs. Kennedy was the target of a certain amount of hate mail throughout her public life. During her marriage to Onassis, she had round-the-clock protection:

"I guess the theme song of my life is that oldie 'Me and My Shadow.'"

MARRIAGE TO ARISTOTLE ONASSIS

After the loss of baby Patrick in 1963, her sister Lee confided in longtime friend Aristotle Onassis. He suggested that Jackie and Lee visit Greece and cruise the islands. He offered to put his yacht, *Christina,* and its crew at their disposal. They could bring friends and travel wherever they wished. He offered to remain ashore or out of sight, whichever they preferred. Mrs. Kennedy accepted the invitation but insisted that Ari accompany them: "I can't possibly accept this man's hospitality and then not let him come along. It would be too cruel."

In October 1968, Mrs. Kennedy married Onassis. "Jackie, you're going to fall off your pedestal," friends warned her.

"That's better than freezing there," she reportedly replied.

Regarding her remarriage, she told Truman Capote:

"I can't very well marry a dentist from New Jersey."

At the time of her wedding to Onassis, the press landed on the beach at Skorpios. Onassis's seamen met them, and it became obvious that someone might be hurt. The bride-to-be put a halt to the proceedings:

"These men also have to make a living."

On the morning of the wedding, October 20, 1968, an attempt was made to make peace with the media. She wrote to the press:

"We know you understand that even though people may be well known, they still hold in their hearts the emotions of a simple person for the moments that are the most important of those we know on earth—birth, marriage, and death. We wish our wedding to be a private moment among the cypresses of Skorpios with only members of the family present—five of them little children. If you will give us these moments, we will gladly give you all the cooperation possible for you to take the pictures you need."

※

Mrs. Onassis once told a close friend:

"Nobody could understand why I married Ari. But I just couldn't live anymore as the Kennedy widow. It was a release, freedom from the oppressive obsession the world had with me."

※

"Marrying him [Onassis] liberated me from the Kennedys—especially the Kennedy administration. None of them could understand why I'd want that funny, little squiggly name when I used to have the greatest name of all."

※

Speaking of her marriage to Onassis, shortly after Robert Kennedy's assassination:

"I wanted to go away. They were killing Kennedys and I didn't want them to harm my children. I wanted to go off. I wanted to be somewhere safe."

※

Some comments regarding her very wealthy new husband:
  "Ari never stops working. He dreams in millions."

Truman Capote: "I gave a party and my dog chewed up Lee Radziwill's sable coat."
  Jackie said: "Don't worry. We can buy another sable for Lee tomorrow and charge it to Ari. He won't mind."

Her cousin Edie Beale quotes her at the time Onassis saved Edie and her mother from eviction by paying for the repairs on their house on Long Island:
  "Don't you think I'm lucky to be married to such a splendid person?"

For her fortieth birthday, Onassis gave her, among other gems, a pair of "Apollo 11" earrings to celebrate man's walk on the moon. At the party, Greek actress Katina Paxinou sat alongside Mrs. Onassis and complimented her on her new earrings. Two spheres representing Earth and the moon were joined by what was supposed to be a miniature spaceship:
  "Ari was actually apologetic about them. He felt they were such trifles. But he promised me that, if I'm good, next year he'll give me the moon itself."

Regarding Onassis's taste in clothes:
  "Look at him. He must have four hundred suits. But he wears the same

gray one in New York, the same blue one in Paris, and the same brown one in London."

There were many rumors after her marriage to Onassis. She told Truman Capote:

"It's a lie, a complete lie. I don't have any money. When I married Ari, my income from the Kennedy estate stopped and so did my widow's pension from the U.S. government. I didn't make any premarital financial agreement with Ari. I know it's an old Greek custom, but I couldn't do it. I didn't want to barter myself. Except for my personal possessions, I have exactly five thousand two hundred dollars in a bank account. Everything else I charge to Olympic Airways."

To a friend she complained:

"You know, everyone talks about how rich I am. I'm not really that rich. I have a few thousand in my checking account, some savings, a few stocks and bonds." Then she added, "Of course there are a lot of things I can charge to Olympic Airways."

In 1975, when Onassis was very ill, Mrs. Onassis flew to Athens with Dr. Isidore Rosenfeld, a heart specialist. She was firm on having her husband moved to Paris:

"He's my husband and I believe this switch is necessary. Let's not argue about it."

In Athens after Onassis's funeral, she gave a short statement to the press:

"Aristotle Onassis rescued me at a time when my life was engulfed in shadows. He meant a lot to me. He brought me into a world where one could find both happiness and love. We lived through many beautiful experiences together which cannot be forgotten, and for which I will be eternally grateful....Nothing has changed both with Aristotle's sisters and his daughter. The same love binds us as when he lived."

She returned to Greece to dedicate a new wing of a children's camp in memory of Onassis:

"My main purpose for coming to Greece, apart from loving the country, is to put into practice the last instructions of my late husband in order to preserve his name."

ON HER OWN AGAIN

Life in New York

In February 1964, while still living in Washington, Mrs. Kennedy spent a weekend at the Hotel Carlyle in New York and said that for the first time in months she felt "like a human being—I can walk the streets and not be singled out."

After being widowed twice by the age of forty-five, she confided to a friend:

"I have always lived through men. Now I realize I can't do that anymore."

After the death of Onassis, she had a number of prominent escorts, one of whom was Mike Nichols.

"Taking you anyplace is like going out with a national monument," he once said.

"Yes," Mrs. Onassis retorted, "but isn't it fun?"

After a dinner party in New York, she left with Mr. and Mrs. Bertrand Taylor, who lived just a few blocks north of Mrs. Onassis on Fifth Avenue and offered her a lift home. She accepted, and when Mr. Taylor went outside to get the car, he noticed two men with cameras standing in the shadows. As he went back inside, he said, "I think I'd better warn you that there are two photographers outside."

With a look of mock anguish, she replied, "Only two? I must be slipping!" With a wink she added, "Let's have some fun with them."

Smiling, she put her hand in the crook of Taylor's elbow and walked out onto the sidewalk with him.

Paris Match correspondent Benno Graziani knew Federico Fellini well. Once when Fellini was in New York, he asked if Benno could arrange for him to meet Mrs. Onassis. When they were dining together, she spoke in detail of Fellini's work. Benno commented to her, "I didn't know you were so familiar with Fellini's work."

She replied, "When I knew he was coming for dinner, I watched all his films and read practically all the books written about him."

A few years ago friends gave a small dinner party for two mutual friends who had just married, and Mrs. Onassis was there. The next day the hosts received a handwritten letter:

"How could there be an evening more magical than last night? Everyone is enhanced and touched by being with two people just discovering how much they love each other. I have known and adored him for so long, always wishing he would find happiness....Seeing him with her and getting to know her, I see he has at last—and she so exceptional, whom you describe so movingly, has too. I am so full of joy for both—I just kept thinking about it all day today. What wonderful soothing hosts you are—

what a dazzling gathering of their friends—in that beautiful tower, with New York glittering below."

※

In New York in the early 1970s, when her maid had the day off, Mrs. Kennedy would answer the phone in a fake Spanish accent in hopes callers wouldn't recognize her voice:

"I have to do that to get rid of people."

※

Mrs. Onassis liked to people-watch:

"Think of the plots that are being hatched down there," she said, looking down from the balcony of the Four Seasons restaurant.

Or at lunch at Les Pleiades:

"What do you suppose they're buying and selling over their cold sea bass?"

※

Over lunch, André Previn asked her whether it bothered her that people looked at her:

"That's why I always wear my dark glasses. It may be that they're looking at me, but none of them can ever tell which ones I'm looking back at. That way I can have fun with it!"

※

During her years in New York, Mrs. Onassis became involved in the fight to save Grand Central Station:

"We've heard that it's too late to save this station, but that's not true.

Even at the eleventh hour you can succeed, and I think that's exactly what we'll do. I care desperately about saving old buildings."

Kent L. Barwich, president, Municipal Art Society, quoted Mrs. Onassis concerning the proposed Columbus Circle building, which would have been the tallest in the world:

"They're stealing the sky."

Self-Image

Although shy and introverted as a young girl, over the years she developed confidence in her own style and viewpoint.

On May 25, 1972, she told the *Scranton Times:*

"Why do people always try to see me through the different names I have had at different times? People often forget that I was Jacqueline Bouvier before being Mrs. Kennedy or Mrs. Onassis. Throughout my life I have always tried to remain true to myself. This I will continue to do as long as I live."

"The trouble with me is I'm an outsider. And that's a very hard thing to be in American life."

"I have a tendency to go into a downward spiral of depression or isolation when I'm sad. To go out, to take a walk, to take a swim, that's very much what the Kennedys do. It's a salvation, really."

"I'm solitary. I'm rather introverted. I'm really glad my children have a sense of humor—I think I'm a bit irreverent."

✻

"I am happiest when I'm alone."

✻

Asked by poet Stephen Spender at a 1979 dinner party to name her proudest accomplishment, she answered:

"Well, I think my biggest achievement is that, after going through a rather difficult time, I consider myself comparatively sane."

Philosophy of Life

In March 1961, she said:

"Happiness is not where you think you find it. I'm determined not to worry. So many people poison every day worrying about the next. I've learned a lot from my husband."

✻

Robert Kennedy quoted Jacqueline Kennedy after she returned from the funeral of Martin Luther King, Jr. in April 1968:

"Of course people feel guilty for a moment. But they hate feeling guilty. They can't stand it for very long. Then they turn."

✻

Bruce Tracy, an editor at Doubleday, once had a chance to go to Europe but would have to miss some events regarding the publication of a book they

were both working on. He asked Jackie's advice, and she said:
"Life comes first."

✻

Joan Kennedy said after the death of a man she might have married after her divorce from Ted Kennedy, "When does the heartache end? I finally meet a decent man and he's taken from me. It's just not fair."

Mrs. Onassis replied:

"Joan, do you really expect life to be fair after everything we've gone through? It's up to you to take what happiness you can find. And you have to soldier on, whether you like it or not."

✻

Longtime friend Viviana Crespi remembers that her son adored Mrs. Onassis. He'd sent her his poems, and she replied:

"You must continue. Poets are the ones who change the world."

✻

In 1994:

"I have been through a lot and I have suffered a great deal. But I have had lots of happy moments, as well. Every moment one lives is different from the other. The good, the bad, hardship, the joy, the tragedy, love, and happiness are all interwoven into one single, indescribable whole that is called life. You cannot separate the good from the bad. And perhaps there is no need to do so, either."

Work

In 1975, when her old friend Letitia Baldridge made the suggestion, she replied:

"Who me—*work?*"

In an interview with *Ms.* magazine, March 1979, she discussed her work:

"Before I was married, I worked on a newspaper. Being a journalist seemed the ideal way of both having a job and experiencing the world, especially for anyone with a sense of adventure. I wouldn't choose it as a profession now—journalism has variety, but doesn't allow you to enter different worlds in depth, as book publishing does—though I understand why so many young people are attracted to it. Being a reporter seems a ticket out to the world.

"If I hadn't married, I might have had a life very much like Gloria Emerson's. She is a friend who started out in Paris writing about fashion— and then ended up as a correspondent in Vietnam. The two ends of her career couldn't seem farther apart, and that is the virtue of journalism. You never know where it's going to take you, but it can be a noble life—she became a correspondent and an author of influence.

"What has been sad for many women of my generation is that they weren't supposed to work if they had families. There they were, with the highest education, and what were they to do when the children were grown—watch the raindrops coming down the windowpane? Leave their fine minds unexercised? Of course women should work if they want to. You have to be doing something you enjoy. That is a definition of happiness: 'complete use of one's faculties along lines leading to excellence in a life affording them scope.' It applies to women as well as to men. We can't all reach it, but we can try to reach it to some degree.

"No, I don't get questioned about my salary or why I work. At least, I've never felt that kind of resentment. Perhaps it's just that the people who resent my working say it to everyone else—but not to me.

"I think that people who work themselves have respect for the work of others. I remember a taxi driver who took me to the office. He said, 'Lady, you work and you don't *have* to?' I said yes. He turned around and said, 'I think that's great!'"

Books

Jacqueline Bouvier Kennedy Onassis had a lifelong love of reading, long before she began her career in book publishing.

Books for grown-ups were kept in the guest room where Jacqueline took her afternoon naps as a child.

One day she remarked, "Mummy, I liked the story of the lady and the dog."

Her mother discovered that Jacqueline had been reading a book of short stories by Chekhov with sophisticated plots and elaborate Russian names.

"Did you understand all the words?" her mother asked.

"Yes—except what's a midwife?" replied Jacqueline.

"Didn't you mind all those long names?"

"No, why should I mind?" asked the six-year-old Jacqueline.

✳

She came to love and know most about the eighteenth century. She wrote:

"When you read a lot you come across some things that interest you more than others. So you read a little bit more about those things that interest you. I was fascinated by what I read about the eighteenth century period and as I dug deeper I became more fascinated. First thing I knew, I wanted to know everything I could about the period."

During December 1960, she accompanied her husband to the family's home in Palm Beach, she to recuperate from the birth of John F. Kennedy Jr. and he to recuperate from the rigors of the presidential campaign. She wrote to Kenneth Galbraith:

"Jack read Robert Walpole in one night. It has taken me two weeks to finish [Archibald] MacLeish and [John] Betjeman—isn't that awful....I can't tell you the peace they have brought me, reading them at night, in these days when I have to fuss with things like mail and evening dresses all day."

Her last interview was with John F. Baker, the British-born editor of *Publishers Weekly,* a little more than a year before her death:

"I love books. I've known writers all my life.

"I'm drawn to books that are out of our regular experience. Books of other cultures, ancient histories. I'm interested in the arts in general, especially the creative process. I'm fascinated by hearing artists talk about their craft. To me, a wonderful book is one that takes me on a journey into something I didn't know before."

She enjoyed reading history:

"If you live through a time, it crystallizes later for you. You want to know more about it.

"If you produce one book, you will have done something wonderful in your life."

Jacqueline Kennedy Onassis, Editor

After the death of Aristotle Onassis, she returned to New York. She joined Viking in 1975 as a consulting editor, moving on to Doubleday in 1977.

"After I got out of college, I wanted to write for a newspaper or work for a publishing house, but I did other things. When the time was right, I did this. I would always have liked to. I see my future as staying on as an editor at Viking, hopefully. I love the work I do."

In an April 19, 1993, interview with John F. Baker of *Publishers Weekly,* she was asked why she had come into publishing:

"For the obvious reasons—I'd majored in literature, I had many friends in publishing, I love books, I've known writers all my life."

Aware that she was not being accepted at first as a professional in the world of publishing, she was defensive:

"It's not as if I've never done anything interesting. I've been a reporter myself and I've lived through important parts of American history. I'm not the worst choice for this position."

Quoted by author Eugene Kennedy, who worked on a book with her:
"Like everybody else," she said good-humoredly, "I have to work my way up to an office with a window."

Mrs. Onassis left Viking in 1977 because of Jeffrey Archer's controversial novel *Shall We Tell the President?* depicting Teddy Kennedy as the target of an assassination attempt. She issued a statement:
"Last spring when told of the book, I tried to separate my lives as a Viking employee and a Kennedy relative. But this fall, when it was suggested that I had had something to do with acquiring the book and that I was not distressed by its publication, I felt I had to resign."

After leaving Viking, she moved on to Doubleday:
"One of the good things about working for a publishing house like Doubleday is its size: somewhere among its different divisions, there is a place for almost every subject and kind of book."

In her interview with John F. Baker of *Publishers Weekly,* she said:
"One of the things I like about publishing is that you don't promote the editor—you promote the book and the author. I have no profound thoughts [on publishing]. But I'm always optimistic that people will buy good books."

As an editor, Mrs. Onassis had a line to draw between the need for publicity and her own reserve. Judith Martin (Miss Manners) covered a book party for *In the Russian Style*, which Mrs. Onassis had edited for Viking Press. The book consisted of photographs of and quotations about imperial Russian society, including their clothes, jewels, lavish parties, marriages, and love affairs, with judgments on same. The reporter asked the former first lady if her "point of view changed about the propriety of examining the private lives of public figures?"

"These things were public," she replied, referring to the sources, including Catherine the Great's love letters. "When it's past, it becomes history." And if a historian someday uses her letters? "I won't be here to mind."

On her work as an editor specializing in nonfiction:

"After all, I *have* lived through a lot of American history."

She mentioned that ballerina Gelsey Kirkland was working on a series of books about a girl learning to be a ballerina:

"Young girls are always fascinated either by ballet or horses. I was fascinated by both."

Mimi Kazon, a former political columnist, met Jackie at a book party and agreed to send her a packet of her best material for possible publication by Doubleday. A few months later she received a call:

"This is Jackie Onassis of Doubleday. I received your columns and found them quick and witty. But they were all about power, and frankly I'm not into power."

In 1979, she wrote Louis Auchincloss urging him to collaborate with French photographer Deborah Turbeville on a book about the Palace of Versailles:

"Only a writer at home in the period could do such a text and that is why I thought of you. I can just picture popping you down in the Galerie des Glaces and I can imagine what you would say to everyone there."

The book, *The Unseen Versailles,* was published in 1982.

New York, 1979:

"That is part of an editor's job. You keep asking everyone—friends, authors, agents, experts; anyone with access to a particular world—if they know of a person who should be published or a subject that should be treated."

Jacqueline Onassis was the editor for *Maverick in Mauve,* the diary of Adele Sloane, brought to her by her cousin by marriage Louis Auchincloss, whose wife was Adele Sloane's granddaughter:

"I saw a great deal in it. What was so moving to me was the spirit of this woman, and the dignity with which she lived her life, and her basic character. You think of the mauve decade and all their extravagances, their private trains, the jewels, the weddings, and then you realize that she would have to live through terrible troubles as well. That her life would seem to be ideal and then tragedy would strike her—losing her child, for example.

And that her life was not going to be so perfect after all, that she would have enormous difficulties but somehow her spirit and her character would carry her through. You realize, especially when she writes so movingly about the death of her child, how difficult her life could be.

"I'm hoping it will reach a very wide audience."

She had worked closely with Louis Auchincloss on the above-mentioned *Maverick in Mauve* and overruled his desire for chronological accuracy, saying:

"Oh, Louis, don't be such a Ph.D."

"What I like about being an editor is that it expands your knowledge and heightens your discrimination. Each book takes you down another path. Hopefully, some of them move people and some of them do some good.

"Editing *The Firebird and Other Russian Fairy Tales* for Viking meant working with a Russian translator and doing research in the New York Public Library's Slavonic room."

On *The Cartoon History of the Universe,* a comic-book paperback by Larry Gonick:

"It's very accurate, and a much better account of how civilization developed than many more serious ones I've read."

❊

An editor mentioned during a meeting that he was trying to get a Hunter Thompson book. Sitting next to him, she slipped him a note:

"I would give up food to publish Hunter Thompson."

Working with Muffie (Mrs. Henry) Brandon on *Remember the Ladies* for Viking in 1976, they discovered that there was a root that women chewed to induce abortions. Mrs. Onassis said:

"Put that in—we want the book to be factual, and also earthy."

She had concern about a section on the role of women in marriage:

"We don't want the book to be a liberationist tract."

They found a letter from Martha Washington describing Georgetown as "a dirty hole."

Mrs. Onassis laughed and commented, "It still is."

In 1982, she wrote to Louis Auchincloss regarding his book *False Dawn,* a collection of portraits of seventeenth-century women:

"The most uncomfortable thing I have ever had to do is edit your immaculate writing. I hope and expect that you will object vociferously and that I will learn a lot from you in the process.

"Please realize that one gets obsessive and nit picking when editing a manuscript filled with facts, in a concentrated session. I did yours in a day and a night in Martha's Vineyard. It isn't at all like reading a book for pleasure and I may have been overzealous."

On Her Own Again

In her April 19, 1993, interview with John F. Baker of *Publishers Weekly:*

Egyptian Nobel Prize–winning novelist Naguib Mahfouz was published by Bantam, Doubleday, Dell:

"When I read in the paper that this Egyptian had won the Nobel Prize, I thought, 'We've got to have that.' I've always loved the cultures of the Mediterranean, and I'd lived in Greece, and it clicked with some other Mediterranean writers I very much admired—Kazantzakis, for instance."

On Mahfouz's *Cairo Trilogy,* she showed off the covers:

"Aren't they lovely? These were designed by Alex Gottfryd [the late Doubleday art director]. See how each cover has an antique photograph from a different era, reflecting the book's contents?"

John Russell, former chief art critic of the *New York Times,* recalls his ambition to write something that would last—forever—as a thank-you letter to the U.S. The idea began to collapse under its own weight. Mrs. Onassis said:

"Don't let's talk anymore about that book you're never going to write."

In a July 21, 1994, *Publishers Weekly* article by author Elizabeth Crook, whose books Mrs. Onassis edited, she advised:

"Don't allow yourself to be repetitious or sentimental. It backfires."

In 1993 she said:

"I certainly don't think dealing with authors and agents is very hard. I don't work with agents as much as some editors, perhaps—though sometimes, when something crosses their desk, I hope they think of me and say, 'Oh, she might like that.'"

❊

Mrs. Onassis urged society columnist Suzy (Aileen Mehle) to write a book:

"You know these people like no one else. Write about them, their lives, their ambitions, their lies. Write how nothing *really* is the way it seems. How these women who seem to have it all are really desperate and trapped."

Then she would smile and say:

"But if one has to be trapped and unhappy, maybe it's better in sables after all."

(Although her taste never ran to sables.)

On Writing Her Memoirs

On her place in history:

"So many people hit the White House with their Dictaphone running....I never even kept a journal. I thought, 'I want to live my life, not record it.'"

❊

Doubleday's deputy publisher Bill Barry, who worked with her for many years, suggested she write her memoirs. She said that life is too precious:

"I want to savor it. I'd rather spend my time feeling a galloping horse, or the mist of the ocean up at Martha's Vineyard."

❊

Author David Wise saw her about two years before her death and asked her when she would write her own book. She laughed and replied:

"Maybe when I'm ninety."

She said that people change and the person she would have written about thirty years ago "is not the same person today. The imagination takes over. When Isak Dinesen wrote *Out of Africa,* she left out how badly her husband had treated her. She created a new past, in effect. And why sit indoors with a yellow pad writing a memoir when you could be outdoors?"

He asked her how she managed to deal with the tabloids:

"The river of sludge will go on and on. It isn't about me."

In spite of the fact that there have been twenty-two biographies about her, and there are more article entries under her name in the *Readers' Guide to Periodical Literature* than for any other living American woman, she has never spoken to more than one or two of those reporters and authors.

She told friend Jayne Wrightsman about two years before she died:

"I'm sixty-two now, and I've been in the public eye for more than thirty years. I can't believe that anybody still cares about me or is still interested in what I do."

Maurice Tempelsman

Belgian-born financier and diamond merchant Maurice Tempelsman was her companion over the last years of her life. Dignified, intellectual, and charming, Tempelsman had first met the Kennedys in the 1950s. Starting as a friend, he later became her financial adviser, increasing her fortune considerably. Along with a shared love of art and antiques, they spent quiet times sailing on his yacht, bird-watching, and strolling in Central Park.

"I admire Maurice's strength and his success. I truly hope my notoriety doesn't force him out of my life."

Shortly before her death, she wrote notes to her children. To John, she wrote:

"I understand the pressure you'll forever have to endure as a Kennedy, even though we brought you into this world as an innocent. You, especially, have a place in history.

"No matter what course in life you choose, all I can ask is that you and Caroline continue to make me, the Kennedy family and yourself proud.

"Stay loyal to those who love you. Especially Maurice [Tempelsman]. He's a decent man with an abundance of common sense. You will do well to seek his advice."

Grandchildren

On July 19, 1986, Caroline Kennedy married Edwin Schlossberg. Their first child, daughter Rose, was born June 25, 1988, at New York Hospital–Cornell Medical Center.

In the spring of 1988, Mrs. Onassis's common refrain to friends was:

"I'm going to be a grandmother—imagine that."

About her grandchildren (Rose, now six; Tatiana, three; and Jack, sixteen months):

"They make my spirits soar!"

To Caroline, she wrote:

"The children have been a wonderful gift to me and I'm thankful to have once again seen our world through their eyes. They restore my faith in the family's future. You and Ed have been so wonderful to share them with me so unselfishly."

THE FINAL CHAPTER

Her Illness

In February of 1994, it was announced that Mrs. Onassis had been diagnosed with non-Hodgkin's lymphoma. Treated with radiation and chemotherapy (and emergency surgery for a bleeding ulcer in April), her cancer outpaced the oncologists. Released from New York Hospital–Cornell Medical Center, she returned to her apartment, where she passed away Thursday, May 19, 1994.

John F. Kennedy Jr. made a statement to the press the next morning:

"Last night, at around ten-fifteen, my mother passed on. She was surrounded by her friends and her family and her books and the people and the things that she loved.

"And she did it in her own way and in her own terms, and we all feel lucky for that and now she's in God's hands.

"There's been an enormous outpouring of good wishes from everyone both in New York and beyond. And I speak for all of our family when we say we're extremely grateful. Everyone's been very generous. And I hope now that, you know, we can just have these next couple of days in relative peace."

After a funeral mass at the Church of St. Ignatius Loyola, she was buried beside President Kennedy at Arlington.

After the diagnosis of her cancer, she spoke to a friend:

"Well, I have to make the best of the situation, and I'm going to do that."

✤

To another friend a few months before she died, when she first knew she was sick:

"But even if I have only five years, so what, I've had a great run."

✤

She spoke about her illness:

"I don't get it. I did everything right to take care of myself and look what happened. Why in the world did I do all those push-ups?"

✤

Just a month before she died, she told a friend that things were going well:

"I'm almost glad it happened because it's given me a second life. I laugh and enjoy things so much more."

Her Will

She left:

"Copyright interest in personal papers, letters or other writings by me including any royalties" and "all tangible personal property including, without limitation, my collection of letters, papers and documents, my personal effects, my furniture, furnishings, rugs, pictures, books, silver, plates, linen, china, glassware, objects of art, wearing apparel, jewelry, automobiles and their accessories and all other household goods to my children."

✤

The Final Chapter

Her final request was to ask Caroline and John to protect her privacy after her death:

"I request but do not direct my children to respect my wish for privacy, with respect to…papers, letters and writings…[and] take whatever action is warranted to prevent [their] display, publication or distribution."